# Introduction to R for Quantitative Finance

Solve a diverse range of problems with R, one of the most powerful tools for quantitative finance

**Gergely Daróczi**

**Michael Puhle**

**Edina Berlinger**

**Péter Csóka**

**Dániel Havran**

**Márton Michaletzky**

**Zsolt Tulassay**

**Kata Váradi**

**Agnes Vidovics-Dancs**

BIRMINGHAM - MUMBAI

# Introduction to R for Quantitative Finance

First published: November 2013

Production Reference: 1151113

Published by Packt Publishing Ltd.
Livery Place
35 Livery Street
Birmingham B3 2PB, UK..

ISBN 978-1-78328-093-3

www.packtpub.com

Cover Image by Suresh Mogre (suresh.mogre.99@gmail.com)

# Credits

# About the Authors

**Gergely Daróczi** is a Ph.D. candidate in Sociology with around eight years' experience in data management and analysis tasks within the R programming environment. Besides teaching Statistics at different Hungarian universities and doing data analysis jobs for several years, Gergely has founded and coordinated a UK-based online reporting startup company recently. This latter software or platform as a service which is called *rapporter.net* will potentially provide an intuitive frontend and an interface to all the methods and techniques covered in the book. His role in the book was to provide R implementation of the QF problems and methods.

I am more than grateful to the members of my little family for their support and understanding, even though they missed me a lot while I worked on the R parts of this book. I am also really thankful to all the co-authors who teach at the Corvinus University of Budapest, Hungary, for providing useful content for this co-operation.

**Michael Puhle** obtained a Ph.D. in Finance from the University of Passau in Germany. He worked for several years as a Senior Risk Controller at Allianz Global Investors in Munich, and as an Assistant Manager at KPMG's Financial Risk Management practice, where he was advising banks on market risk models. Michael is also the author of *Bond Portfolio Optimization* published by *Springer Publishing*.

**Edina Berlinger** has a Ph.D. in Economics from the Corvinus University of Budapest. She is an Associate Professor, teaching corporate finance, investments, and financial risk management. She is the Head of Department for Finance of the university and is also the Chair of the Finance Sub committee the Hungarian Academy of Sciences. Her expertise covers student loan systems, risk management, and, recently, network analysis. She has led several research projects in student loan design, liquidity management, heterogeneous agent models, and systemic risk.

**Péter Csóka** is an Associate Professor at the Department of Finance, Corvinus University of Budapest, and a research fellow in the Game Theory Research Group, Centre For Economic and Regional Studies, Hungarian Academy of Sciences. He received his Ph.D. in Economics from Maastricht University in 2008. His research topics include risk measures, risk capital allocation, game theory, corporate finance, and general equilibrium theory. He is currently focused on analyzing risk contributions for systemic risk and for illiquid portfolios. He has papers published in journals such as *Mathematical Methods of Operational Research*, *European Journal of Operational Research*, *Games and Economic Behaviour*, and *Journal of Banking and Finance*. He is the Chair of the organizing committee of the Annual Financial Market Liquidity Conference in Budapest.

**Daniel Havran** is a Post Doctoral Fellow at the Institute of Economics, Centre for Economic and Regional Studies, Hungarian Academy of Sciences. He also holds a part-time Assistant Professorship position at the Corvinus University of Budapest, where he teaches Corporate Finance (BA and Ph.D. levels), and Credit Risk Management (MSc) courses. He obtained his Ph.D. in Economics at Corvinus University of Budapest in 2011. His research interests are corporate cash, funding liquidity management, and credit derivatives over-the-counter markets.

**Márton Michaletzky** obtained his Ph.D. degree in Economics in 2011 from Corvinus University of Budapest. Between 2000 and 2003, he has been a Risk Manager and Macroeconomic Analyst with Concorde Securities Ltd. As Capital Market Transactions Manager, he gained experience in an EUR 3 bn securitization at the Hungarian State Motorway Management Company. In 2012, he took part in the preparation of an IPO and the private placement of a Hungarian financial services provider. Prior to joining DBH Investment, he was an assistant professor at the Department of Finance of CUB.

**Zsolt Tulassay** works as a Quantitative Analyst at a major US investment bank, validating derivatives pricing models. Previously, Zsolt worked as an Assistant Lecturer at the Department of Finance at Corvinus University, teaching courses on Derivatives, Quantitative Risk Management, and Financial Econometrics. Zsolt holds MA degrees in Economics from Corvinus University of Budapest and Central European University. His research interests include derivatives pricing, yield curve modeling, liquidity risk, and heterogeneous agent models.

**Kata Váradi** is an Assistant Professor at the Department of Finance, Corvinus University of Budapest since 2013. Kata graduated in Finance in 2009 from Corvinus University of Budapest, and was awarded a Ph.D. degree in 2012 for her thesis on the analysis of the market liquidity risk on the Hungarian stock market. Her research areas are market liquidity, fixed income securities, and networks in healthcare systems. Besides doing research, she is active in teaching as well. She teaches mainly Corporate Finance, Investments, Valuation, and Multinational Financial Management.

**Agnes Vidovics-Dancs** is a Ph.D. candidate and an Assistant Professor at the Department of Finance, Corvinus University of Budapest. Previously, she worked as a Junior Risk Manager in the Hungarian Government Debt Management Agency. Her main research areas are government debt management in general, especially sovereign crises and defaults.

# About the Reviewers

**Dr. Hari Shanker Gupta** is a Quantitative Research Analyst working in the area of Algorithming Trading System Development. Prior to this, he was a Post Doctoral Fellow at Indian Institute of Science (IISc), Bangalore, India. Hari has pursued his Ph.D. from Department of Mathematics, IISc, in the field of Applied Mathematics and Scientific Computation in the year 2010. Hari had completed his M.Sc. in Mathematics from Banaras Hindu University (B.H.U.), Varanasi, India. During M.Sc., Hari was awarded four gold medals for his outstanding performance in B.H.U., Varanasi.

Hari has published five research papers in reputed journals in the field of Mathematics and Scientific Computation. He has experience of working in the areas of mathematics, statistics, and computations. These include the topics: numerical methods, partial differential equation, mathematical finance, stochastic calculus, data analysis, finite difference, and finite element method. He is very comfortable with the mathematics software, Matlab; the statistics programming language, R, and, the programming language, C, and has been recently working on the Python platform.

**Ronald Hochreiter** is an Assistant Professor at the Department of Finance, Accounting and Statistics, at the WU Vienna University of Economics and Business. He obtained his Ph.D. in Computational Management Science at the University of Vienna in 2005. He is an avid R user and develops R packages mainly for optimization modeling purposes as well as for applications in Finance. A summary of his R projects can be found at `http://www.hochreiter.net/R/`, and some of his tutorials on Financial Engineering with R are online at `http://www.finance-r.com/`.

# www.PacktPub.com

## Support files, eBooks, discount offers and more

You might want to visit www.PacktPub.com for support files and downloads related to your book.

Did you know that Packt offers eBook versions of every book published, with PDF and ePub files available? You can upgrade to the eBook version at www.PacktPub.com and as a print book customer, you are entitled to a discount on the eBook copy. Get in touch with us at service@packtpub.com for more details.

At www.PacktPub.com, you can also read a collection of free technical articles, sign up for a range of free newsletters and receive exclusive discounts and offers on Packt books and eBooks.

http://PacktLib.PacktPub.com

Do you need instant solutions to your IT questions? PacktLib is Packts online digital book library. Here, you can access, read and search across Packt's entire library of books.

## Why Subscribe?
- Fully searchable across every book published by Packt
- Copy and paste, print and bookmark content
- On demand and accessible via web browser

## Free Access for Packt account holders

If you have an account with Packt at www.PacktPub.com, you can use this to access PacktLib today and view nine entirely free books. Simply use your login credentials for immediate access.

# Table of Contents

# Preface

*Introduction to R for Quantitative Finance* will show you how to solve real-world quantitative finance problems using the statistical computing languages R and QF. In this book, we will cover diverse topics ranging from Time Series Analysis to Financial Networks. Each chapter will briefly present the theory and deal with solving a specific problem using R.

## What this book covers

*Chapter 1, Time Series Analysis* (Michael Puhle), explains working with time series data in R. Furthermore, you will learn how to model and forecast house prices, improve hedge ratios using cointegration, and model volatility.

*Chapter 2, Portfolio Optimization* (Péter Csóka, Ferenc Illés, Gergely Daróczi), covers the theoretical idea behind portfolio selection and shows how to apply this knowledge to real-world data.

*Chapter 3, Asset Pricing Models* (Kata Váradi, Barbara Mária Dömötör, Gergely Daróczi), builds on the previous chapter and presents models for the relationship between asset return and risk. We'll cover the Capital Asset Pricing Model and the Arbitrage Pricing Theory.

*Chapter 4, Fixed Income Securities* (Márton Michaletzky, Gergely Daróczi), deals with the basics of fixed income instruments. Furthermore, you will learn how to calculate the risk of such an instrument and construct portfolios that will be immune to changes in interest rates.

*Chapter 5, Estimating the Term Structure of Interest Rates* (Tamás Makara, Gergely Daróczi), introduces the concept of a yield curve and shows how to estimate it using prices of government bonds.

*Chapter 6, Derivatives Pricing* (Ágnes Vidovics-Dancs, Gergely Daróczi), explains the pricing of derivatives using discrete and continuous time models. Furthermore, you will learn how to calculate derivatives risk measures and the so-called "Greeks".

*Chapter 7, Credit Risk Management* (Dániel Havran, Gergely Daróczi), gives an introduction to the credit default models and shows how to model correlated defaults using copulas.

*Chapter 8, Extreme Value Theory* (Zsolt Tulassay), presents possible uses of Extreme Value Theory in insurance and finance. You will learn how to fit a model to the tails of the distribution of fire losses. Then we will use the fitted model to calculate Value-at-Risk and Expected Shortfall.

*Chapter 9, Financial Networks* (Edina Berlinger, Gergely Daróczi), explains how financial networks can be represented, simulated, visualized, and analyzed in R. We will analyze the interbank lending market and learn how to systemically detect important financial institutions.

# What you need for this book

All the code examples provided in this book should be run in the R console that is to be installed first on a computer. You can download the software for free and find the installation instructions for all major operating systems at http://r-project. org. Although we will not cover advanced topics such as how to use R in Integrated Development Environments, there are awesome plugins for Emacs, Eclipse, vi, or Notepad++ besides other editors, and we can also highly recommend trying RStudio, which is a free and open source IDE dedicated to R.

Apart from a working R installation, we will also use some user-contributed R packages that can be easily installed from the Comprehensive R Archive Network. To install a package, use the install.packages command in the R console, shown as follows:

```
> install.packages('zoo')
```

After installation, the package should be also loaded first to the current R session before usage:

```
> library(zoo)
```

You can find free introductory articles and manuals on the R homepage, but this book is targeted towards beginners, so no additional R knowledge is assumed from the reader.

# Who this book is for

The book is aimed at readers who wish to use R to solve problems in quantitative finance. Some familiarity with finance is assumed, but we generally provide the financial theory as well. Familiarity with R is not assumed. Those who want to get started with R may find this book useful as we don't give a complete overview of the R language but show how to use parts of it to solve specific problems. Even if you already use R, you will surely be amazed to see the wide range of problems that it can be applied to.

# Conventions

In this book, you will find a number of styles of text that distinguish between different kinds of information. Here are some examples of these styles, and an explanation of their meaning.

Code words in text, database table names, folder names, filenames, file extensions, pathnames, dummy URLs, user input, and Twitter handles are shown as follows: "we will employ some methods from the `forecast` package"

A block of R code (usually a function's body) is set as follows:

```
logreturn <- function(x) {
    log(tail(x, -1) / head(x, -1))
}
```

When we wish to draw your attention to a particular part of a code block, the relevant lines or items are set in bold:

```
logreturn <- function(x) {
    log(tail(x, -1) / head(x, -1))
}
```

Any command-line input or output is written as follows:

```
> pi
[1] 3.141593
```

Where ">" shows that the R console is waiting for commands to be evaluated. Multiline expressions are started with the same symbol on the first line, but all the rest lines have a "+" sign at the beginning to show that the last R expression is still to be finished.

**New terms** and **important words** are shown in bold. Words that you see on the screen, in menus or dialog boxes for example, appear in the text like this: "clicking the **Next** button moves you to the next screen".

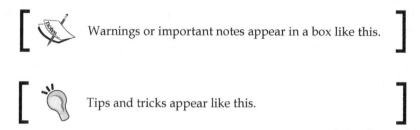

Warnings or important notes appear in a box like this.

Tips and tricks appear like this.

# Reader feedback

Feedback from our readers is always welcome. Let us know what you think about this book—what you liked or may have disliked. Reader feedback is important for us to develop titles that you really get the most out of.

To send us general feedback, simply send an e-mail to feedback@packtpub.com, and mention the book title via the subject of your message.

If there is a topic that you have expertise in and you are interested in either writing or contributing to a book, see our author guide on www.packtpub.com/authors.

# Customer support

Now that you are the proud owner of a Packt book, we have a number of things to help you to get the most from your purchase.

# Downloading the example code

You can download the example code files for all Packt books you have purchased from your account at http://www.packtpub.com. If you purchased this book elsewhere, you can visit http://www.packtpub.com/support and register to have the files e-mailed directly to you.

# Errata

Although we have taken every care to ensure the accuracy of our content, mistakes do happen. If you find a mistake in one of our books—maybe a mistake in the text or the code—we would be grateful if you would report this to us. By doing so, you can save other readers from frustration and help us improve subsequent versions of this book. If you find any errata, please report them by visiting http://www.packtpub.com/submit-errata, selecting your book, clicking on the **errata submission form** link, and entering the details of your errata. Once your errata are verified, your submission will be accepted and the errata will be uploaded on our website, or added to any list of existing errata, under the Errata section of that title. Any existing errata can be viewed by selecting your title from http://www.packtpub.com/support.

# Piracy

Piracy of copyright material on the Internet is an ongoing problem across all media. At Packt, we take the protection of our copyright and licenses very seriously. If you come across any illegal copies of our works, in any form, on the Internet, please provide us with the location address or website name immediately so that we can pursue a remedy.

Please contact us at copyright@packtpub.com with a link to the suspected pirated material.

We appreciate your help in protecting our authors, and our ability to bring you valuable content.

# Questions

You can contact us at questions@packtpub.com if you are having a problem with any aspect of the book, and we will do our best to address it.

# 1
# Time Series Analysis

Time series analysis is concerned with the analysis of data collected over time. Adjacent observations are typically dependent. Time series analysis hence deals with techniques for the analysis of this dependence.

The objective of this chapter is to introduce some common modeling techniques by means of specific applications. We will see how to use R to solve these real-world examples. We begin with some thoughts about how to store and process time series data in R. Afterwards, we deal with linear time series analysis and how it can be used to model and forecast house prices. In the subsequent section, we use the notion of cointegration to improve on the basic minimal variance hedge ratio by taking long-run trends into consideration. The chapter concludes with a section on how to use volatility models for risk management purposes.

## Working with time series data

The native R classes suitable for storing time series data include `vector`, `matrix`, `data.frame`, and `ts` objects. But the types of data that can be stored in these objects are narrow; furthermore, the methods provided by these representations are limited in scope. Luckily, there exist specialized objects that deal with more general representation of time series data: `zoo`, `xts`, or `timeSeries` objects, available from packages of the same name.

It is not necessary to create time series objects for every time series analysis problem, but more sophisticated analyses require time series objects. You could calculate the mean or variance of time series data represented as a vector in R, but if you want to perform a seasonal decomposition using `decompose`, you need to have the data stored in a time series object.

In the following examples, we assume you are working with zoo objects because we think it is one of the most widely used packages. Before we can use zoo objects, we need to install and load the zoo package (if you have already installed it, you only need to load it) using the following command:

```
> install.packages("zoo")
> library("zoo")
```

In order to familiarize ourselves with the available methods, we create a zoo object called aapl from the daily closing prices of Apple's stock, which are stored in the CSV file aapl.csv. Each line on the sheet contains a date and a closing price separated by a comma. The first line contains the column headings (**Date** and **Close**). The date is formatted according to the recommended primary standard notation of ISO 8601 (YYYY-MM-DD). The closing price is adjusted for stock splits, dividends, and related changes.

**Downloading the example code**

You can download the example code files for all Packt books you have purchased from your account at http://www.packtpub.com. If you purchased this book elsewhere, you can visit http://www.packtpub.com/support and register to have the files e-mailed directly to you.

We load the data from our current working directory using the following command:

```
> aapl<-read.zoo("aapl.csv",
+   sep=",", header = TRUE, format = "%Y-%m-%d")
```

To get a first impression of the data, we plot the stock price chart and specify a title for the overall plot (using the main argument) and labels for the x and y axis (using xlab and ylab respectively).

```
> plot(aapl, main = "APPLE Closing Prices on NASDAQ",
+   ylab = "Price (USD)", xlab = "Date")
```

We can extract the first or last part of the time series using the following commands:

```
> head(aapl)
2000-01-03 2000-01-04 2000-01-05 2000-01-06 2000-01-07 2000-01-10
     27.58      25.25      25.62      23.40      24.51      24.08
> tail(aapl)
2013-04-17 2013-04-18 2013-04-19 2013-04-22 2013-04-23 2013-04-24
    402.80     392.05     390.53     398.67     406.13     405.46
```

Apple's all-time high and the day on which it occurred can be found using the following command:

```
> aapl[which.max(aapl)]
2012-09-19
   694.86
```

When dealing with time series, one is normally more interested in returns instead of prices. This is because returns are usually stationary. So we will calculate simple returns or continuously compounded returns (in percentage terms).

```
> ret_simple <- diff(aapl) / lag(aapl, k = -1) * 100
> ret_cont   <- diff(log(aapl)) * 100
```

Summary statistics about simple returns can also be obtained. We use the `coredata` method here to indicate that we are only interested in the stock prices and not the index (dates).

```
> summary(coredata(ret_simple))
     Min.    1st Qu.    Median     Mean    3rd Qu.      Max.
 -51.86000  -1.32500   0.07901   0.12530   1.55300   13.91000
```

The biggest single-day loss is -51.86%. The date on which that loss occurred can be obtained using the following command:

```
> ret_simple[which.min(ret_simple)]
2000-09-29
 -51.85888
```

A quick search on the Internet reveals that the large movement occurred due to the issuance of a profit warning. To get a better understanding of the relative frequency of daily returns, we can plot the histogram. The number of cells used to group the return data can be specified using the `break` argument.

```
> hist(ret_simple, breaks=100, main = "Histogram of Simple Returns",
+   xlab="%")
```

We can restrict our analysis to a subset (a `window`) of the time series. The highest stock price of Apple in 2013 can be found using the following command lines:

```
> aapl_2013 <- window(aapl, start = '2013-01-01', end = '2013-12-31')
> aapl_2013[which.max(aapl_2013)]
2013-01-02
   545.85
```

The quantiles of the return distribution are of interest from a risk-management perspective. We can, for example, easily determine the 1 day 99% Value-at-Risk using a naive historical approach.

```
> quantile(ret_simple, probs = 0.01)
      1%
-7.042678
```

Hence, the probability that the return is below 7% on any given day is only 1%. But if this day occurs (and it will occur approximately 2.5 times per year), 7% is the minimum amount you will lose.

# Linear time series modeling and forecasting

An important class of linear time series models is the family of **Autoregressive Integrated Moving Average (ARIMA)** models, proposed by *Box and Jenkins (1976)*. It assumes that the current value can depend only on the past values of the time series itself or on past values of some error term.

According to Box and Jenkins, building an ARIMA model consists of three stages:

1. Model identification.
2. Model estimation.
3. Model diagnostic checking.

The model identification step involves determining the order (number of past values and number of past error terms to incorporate) of a tentative model using either graphical methods or information criteria. After determining the order of the model, the parameters of the model need to be estimated, generally using either the least squares or maximum likelihood methods. The fitted model must then be carefully examined to check for possible model inadequacies. This is done by making sure the model residuals behave as white noise; that is, there is no linear dependence left in the residuals.

# Modeling and forecasting UK house prices

In addition to the `zoo` package, we will employ some methods from the `forecast` package. If you haven't installed it already, you need to use the following command to do so:

```
> install.packages("forecast")
```

Afterwards, we need to load the class using the following command:

```
> library("forecast")
```

First, we store the monthly house price data (source: Nationwide Building Society) in a `zoo` time series object.

```
> hp <- read.zoo("UKHP.csv", sep = ",",
+    header = TRUE, format = "%Y-%m", FUN = as.yearmon)
```

The `FUN` argument applies the given function (`as.yearmon`, which represents the monthly data points) to the date column. To make sure we really stored monthly data (12 subperiods per period), by specifying `as.yearmon`, we query for the frequency of the data series.

```
> frequency(hp)
[1] 12
```

The result means that we have twelve subperiods (called months) in a period (called year). We again use simple returns for our analysis.

```
> hp_ret <- diff(hp) / lag(hp, k = -1) * 100
```

# Model identification and estimation

We use the `auto.arima` function provided by the `forecast` package to identify the optimal model and estimate the coefficients in one step. The function takes several arguments besides the return series (`hp_ret`). By specifying `stationary = TRUE`, we restrict the search to stationary models. In a similar vein, `seasonal = FALSE` restricts the search to non-seasonal models. Furthermore, we select the Akaike information criteria as the measure of relative quality to be used in model selection.

```
> mod <- auto.arima(hp_ret, stationary = TRUE, seasonal = FALSE,
+    ic="aic")
```

To determine the fitted coefficient values, we query the model output.

```
> mod
Series: hp_ret
ARIMA(2,0,0) with non-zero mean

Coefficients:
         ar1      ar2    intercept
      0.2299   0.3491      0.4345
s.e.  0.0573   0.0575      0.1519

sigma^2 estimated as 1.105:  log likelihood=-390.97
AIC=789.94    AICc=790.1   BIC=804.28
```

An AR(2) process seems to fit the data best, according to Akaike's Information Criteria. For visual confirmation, we can plot the partial autocorrelation function using the command `pacf`. It shows non-zero partial autocorrelations until lag two, hence an AR process of order two seems to be appropriate. The two AR coefficients, the intercept (which is actually the mean if the model contains an AR term), and the respective standard errors are given. In the following example, they are all significant at the 5% level since the respective confidence intervals do not contain zero:

```
> confint(mod)
                2.5 %     97.5 %
ar1         0.1174881 0.3422486
ar2         0.2364347 0.4617421
intercept 0.1368785 0.7321623
```

If the model contains coefficients that are insignificant, we can estimate the model anew using the `arima` function with the `fixed` argument, which takes as input a vector of elements `0` and `NA`. `NA` indicates that the respective coefficient shall be estimated and `0` indicates that the respective coefficient should be set to zero.

## Model diagnostic checking

A quick way to validate the model is to plot time-series diagnostics using the following command:

```
> tsdiag(mod)
```

The output of the preceding command is shown in the following figure:

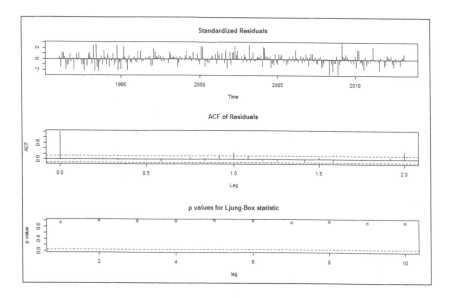

Our model looks good since the standardized residuals don't show volatility clusters, no significant autocorrelations between the residuals according to the ACF plot, and the Ljung-Box test for autocorrelation shows high p-values, so the null hypothesis of independent residuals cannot be rejected.

To assess how well the model represents the data in the sample, we can plot the raw monthly returns (the thin black solid line) versus the fitted values (the thick red dotted line).

```
> plot(mod$x, lty = 1, main = "UK house prices: raw data vs. fitted
+    values", ylab = "Return in percent", xlab = "Date")
> lines(fitted(mod), lty = 2,lwd = 2, col = "red")
```

The output is shown in the following figure:

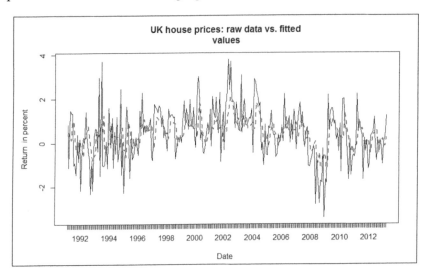

Furthermore, we can calculate common measures of accuracy.

```
> accuracy(mod)
ME        RMSE      MAE        MPE   MAPE   MASE
0.00120   1.0514    0.8059     -Inf  Inf    0.792980241
```

This command returns the mean error, root mean squared error, mean absolute error, mean percentage error, mean absolute percentage error, and mean absolute scaled error.

# Forecasting

To predict the monthly returns for the next three months (April to June 2013), use the following command:

```
> predict(mod, n.ahead=3)
$pred
          Apr        May        Jun
2013 0.5490544  0.7367277  0.5439708

$se
          Apr        May        Jun
2013 1.051422  1.078842  1.158658
```

So we expect a slight increase in the average home prices over the next three months, but with a high standard error of around 1%. To plot the forecast with standard errors, we can use the following command:

```
> plot(forecast(mod))
```

# Cointegration

The idea behind cointegration, a concept introduced by *Granger (1981)* and formalized by *Engle and Granger (1987)*, is to find a linear combination between non-stationary time series that result in a stationary time series. It is hence possible to detect stable long-run relationships between non-stationary time series (for example, prices).

# Cross hedging jet fuel

Airlines are natural buyers of jet fuel. Since the price of jet fuel can be very volatile, most airlines hedge at least part of their exposure to jet fuel price changes. In the absence of liquid jet fuel OTC instruments, airlines use related exchange traded futures contracts (for example, heating oil) for hedging purposes. In the following section, we derive the optimal hedge ratio using first the classical approach of taking into account only the short-term fluctuations between the two prices; afterwards, we improve on the classical hedge ratio by taking into account the long-run stable relationship between the prices as well.

We first load the necessary libraries. The `urca` library has some useful methods for unit root tests and for estimating cointegration relationships.

```
> library("zoo")
> install.packages("urca")
> library("urca")
```

We import the monthly price data for jet fuel and heating oil (in USD per gallon).

```
> prices <- read.zoo("JetFuelHedging.csv", sep = ",",
+    FUN = as.yearmon, format = "%Y-%m", header = TRUE)
```

Taking into account only the short-term behavior (monthly price changes) of the two commodities, one can derive the minimum variance hedge by fitting a linear model that explains changes in jet fuel prices by changes in heating oil prices. The beta coefficient of that regression is the optimal hedge ratio.

```
> simple_mod <- lm(diff(prices$JetFuel) ~ diff(prices$HeatingOil)+0)
```

The function `lm` (for linear model) estimates the coefficients for a best fit of changes in jet fuel prices versus changes in heating oil prices. The `+0` term means that we set the intercept to zero; that is, no cash holdings.

```
> summary(simple_mod)
Call:
lm(formula = diff(prices$JetFuel) ~ diff(prices$HeatingOil) +
    0)
```

```
Residuals:
     Min       1Q    Median       3Q       Max
-0.52503  -0.02968  0.00131  0.03237  0.39602


Coefficients:
                       Estimate Std. Error t value Pr(>|t|)
diff(prices$HeatingOil)  0.89059    0.03983   22.36   <2e-16 ***
---
Signif. codes:  0 '***' 0.001 '**' 0.01 '*' 0.05 '.' 0.1 ' ' 1

Residual standard error: 0.0846 on 189 degrees of freedom
Multiple R-squared:  0.7257,    Adjusted R-squared:  0.7242
F-statistic: 499.9 on 1 and 189 DF,  p-value: < 2.2e-16
```

We obtain a hedge ratio of 0.89059 and a residual standard error of 0.0846. The cross hedge is not perfect; the resulting hedged portfolio is still risky.

We now try to improve on this hedge ratio by using an existing long-run relationship between the levels of jet fuel and heating oil futures prices. You can already guess the existence of such a relationship by plotting the two price series (heating oil prices will be in red) using the following command:

```
> plot(prices$JetFuel, main = "Jet Fuel and Heating Oil Prices",
+    xlab = "Date", ylab = "USD")
> lines(prices$HeatingOil, col = "red")
```

We use Engle and Granger's two-step estimation technique. Firstly, both time series are tested for a unit root (non-stationarity) using the augmented Dickey-Fuller test.

```
> jf_adf <- ur.df(prices$JetFuel, type = "drift")
> summary(jf_adf)
###############################################
# Augmented Dickey-Fuller Test Unit Root Test #
###############################################

Test regression drift


Call:
lm(formula = z.diff ~ z.lag.1 + 1 + z.diff.lag)

Residuals:
     Min       1Q    Median       3Q       Max
-1.06212  -0.05015  0.00566  0.07922  0.38086

Coefficients:
```

```
            Estimate Std. Error t value Pr(>|t|)
(Intercept)  0.03050    0.02177   1.401  0.16283
z.lag.1     -0.01441    0.01271  -1.134  0.25845
z.diff.lag   0.19471    0.07250   2.686  0.00789 **
---
Signif. codes:  0 '***' 0.001 '**' 0.01 '*' 0.05 '.' 0.1 ' ' 1

Residual standard error: 0.159 on 186 degrees of freedom
Multiple R-squared:  0.04099,   Adjusted R-squared:  0.03067
F-statistic: 3.975 on 2 and 186 DF,  p-value: 0.0204


Value of test-statistic is: -1.1335 0.9865

Critical values for test statistics:
      1pct  5pct 10pct
tau2 -3.46 -2.88 -2.57
phi1  6.52  4.63  3.81
```

The null hypothesis of non-stationarity (jet fuel time series contains a unit root) cannot be rejected at the 1% significance level since the test statistic of -1.1335 is not more negative than the critical value of -3.46. The same holds true for heating oil prices (the test statistic is -1.041).

```
> ho_adf <- ur.df(prices$HeatingOil, type = "drift")
> summary(ho_adf)
```

We can now proceed to estimate the static equilibrium model and test the residuals for a stationary time series using an augmented Dickey-Fuller test. Please note that different critical values [for example, from *Engle and Yoo (1987)*] must now be used since the series under investigation is an estimated one.

```
> mod_static <- summary(lm(prices$JetFuel ~ prices$HeatingOil))
> error <- residuals(mod_static)
> error_cadf <- ur.df(error, type = "none")
> summary(error_cadf)
```

The test statistic obtained is -8.912 and the critical value for a sample size of 200 at the 1% level is -4.00; hence we reject the null hypothesis of non-stationarity. We have thus discovered two cointegrated variables and can proceed with the second step; that is, the specification of an **Error-Correction Model (ECM)**. The ECM represents a dynamic model of how (and how fast) the system moves back to the static equilibrium estimated earlier and is stored in the mod_static variable.

```
> djf <- diff(prices$JetFuel)
> dho <- diff(prices$HeatingOil)
> error_lag <- lag(error, k = -1)
> mod_ecm <- lm(djf ~ dho + error_lag)
> summary(mod_ecm)

Call:
lm(formula = djf ~ dho + error_lag + 0)

Residuals:
     Min       1Q    Median        3Q       Max
-0.19158  -0.03246   0.00047   0.02288   0.45117

Coefficients:
          Estimate Std. Error t value Pr(>|t|)
dho        0.90020    0.03238  27.798   <2e-16 ***
error_lag -0.65540    0.06614  -9.909   <2e-16 ***

---

Signif. codes:  0 '***' 0.001 '**' 0.01 '*' 0.05 '.' 0.1 ' ' 1


Residual standard error: 0.06875 on 188 degrees of freedom
Multiple R-squared:  0.8198,    Adjusted R-squared:  0.8179
F-statistic: 427.6 on 2 and 188 DF,  p-value: < 2.2e-16
```

By taking into account the existence of a long-run relationship between jet fuel and heating oil prices (cointegration), the hedge ratio is now slightly higher (0.90020) and the residual standard error significantly lower (0.06875). The coefficient of the error term is negative (-0.65540): large deviations between the two prices are going to be corrected and prices move closer to their long-run stable relationship.

# Modeling volatility

As we saw earlier, ARIMA models are used to model the conditional expectation of a process, given its past. For such a process, the conditional variance is constant. Real-world financial time series exhibit, among other characteristics, volatility clustering; that is, periods of relative calm are interrupted by bursts of volatility.

In this section we look at GARCH time series models that can take this stylized fact of real-world (financial) time series into account and apply these models to VaR forecasting.

# Volatility forecasting for risk management

Financial institutions measure the risk of their activities using a Value-at-Risk (VaR), usually calculated at the 99% confidence level over a 10 business day horizon. This is the loss that is expected to be exceeded only 1% of the time.

We load the zoo library and import monthly return data for Intel Corporation from January 1973 to December 2008.

```
> library("zoo")
> intc <- read.zoo("intc.csv", header = TRUE,
+   sep = ",", format = "%Y-%m", FUN = as.yearmon)
```

## Testing for ARCH effects

A plot of the returns indicates that ARCH effects might exist in the monthly return data.

```
> plot(intc, main = "Monthly returns of Intel Corporation",
+   xlab = "Date", ylab = "Return in percent")
```

The output of the preceding commands is as shown in the following figure:

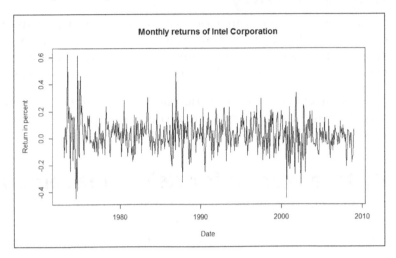

We can use statistical hypothesis tests to verify our inkling. Two commonly used tests are as follows:

- The Ljung-Box test for autocorrelation in squared returns (as a proxy for volatility)
- The **Lagrange Multiplier (LM)** test by *Engle (1982)*

First, we perform the Ljung-Box test on the first 12 lags of the squared returns using the following command:

```
> Box.test(coredata(intc^2), type = "Ljung-Box", lag = 12)

   Box-Ljung test

data:  coredata(intc^2)
X-squared = 79.3451, df = 12, p-value = 5.502e-12
```

We can reject the null hypothesis of no autocorrelations in the squared returns at the 1% significance level. Alternatively, we could employ the LM test from the FinTS package, which gives the same result.

```
> install.packages("FinTS")
> library("FinTS")
> ArchTest(coredata(intc))

   ARCH LM-test; Null hypothesis: no ARCH effects

data:  coredata(intc)
Chi-squared = 59.3647, df = 12, p-value = 2.946e-08
```

Both tests confirm that ARCH effects exist in the monthly Intel returns; hence, an ARCH or GARCH model should be employed in modeling the return time series.

# GARCH model specification

The most commonly used GARCH model, and one that is usually appropriate for financial time series as well, is a GARCH(1,1) model. We use the functions provided by the `rugarch` library for model specification, parameter estimation, backtesting, and forecasting. If you haven't installed the package, use the following command:

```
> install.packages("rugarch")
```

Afterwards, we can load the library using the following command:

```
> library("rugarch")
```

First, we need to specify the model using the function `ugarchspec`. For a GARCH(1,1) model, we need to set the `garchOrder` to `c(1,1)` and the model for the mean (`mean.model`) should be a white noise process and hence equal to `armaOrder = c(0,0)`.

```
> intc_garch11_spec <- ugarchspec(variance.model = list(
+    garchOrder = c(1, 1)),
+    mean.model = list(armaOrder = c(0, 0)))
```

# GARCH model estimation

The actual fitting of the coefficients by the method of maximum likelihood is done by the function `ugarchfit` using the model specification and the return data as inputs.

```
> intc_garch11_fit <- ugarchfit(spec = intc_garch11_spec,
+    data = intc)
```

For additional arguments, see the Help on `ugarchfit`. The output of the fitted model (use the command `intc_garch11_fit`) reveals useful information, such as the values of the optimal parameters, the value of the log-likelihood function, and the information criteria.

# Backtesting the risk model

A useful test for checking the model performance is to do a historical backtest. In a risk model backtest, we compare the estimated VaR with the actual return over the period. If the return is more negative than the VaR, we have a VaR exceedance. In our case, a VaR exceedance should only occur in 1% of the cases (since we specified a 99% confidence level).

The function `ugarchroll` performs a historical backtest on the specified GARCH model (here the model is `intc_garch11_spec`). We specify the backtest as follows:

- The return data to be used is stored in the `zoo` object `intc`
- The start period of the backtest (`n.start`) shall be 120 months after the beginning of the series (that is, January 1983)
- The model should be reestimated every month (`refit.every = 1`)
- We use a `moving` window for the estimation
- We use a `hybrid` solver
- We'd like to calculate the VaR (`calculate.VaR = TRUE`) at the 99% VaR tail level (`VaR.alpha = 0.01`)
- We would like to keep the estimated coefficients (`keep.coef = TRUE`)

The following command shows all the preceding points for a backtest:

```
> intc_garch11_roll <- ugarchroll(intc_garch11_spec, intc,
+    n.start = 120, refit.every = 1, refit.window = "moving",
+    solver = "hybrid", calculate.VaR = TRUE, VaR.alpha = 0.01,
+    keep.coef = TRUE)
```

We can examine the backtesting report using the `report` function. By specifying the `type` argument as `VaR`, the function executes the unconditional and conditional coverage tests for exceedances. `VaR.alpha` is the tail probability and `conf.level` is the confidence level on which the conditional coverage hypothesis test will be based.

```
> report(intc_garch11_roll, type = "VaR", VaR.alpha = 0.01,
+    conf.level = 0.99)
VaR Backtest Report
===========================================
Model:                sGARCH-norm
Backtest Length:    312
Data:


===========================================
alpha:                1%
Expected Exceed:    3.1
Actual VaR Exceed:  5
Actual %:            1.6%


Unconditional Coverage (Kupiec)
Null-Hypothesis:    Correct Exceedances
LR.uc Statistic:    0.968
LR.uc Critical:       6.635
LR.uc p-value:        0.325
```

```
Reject Null:        NO

Conditional Coverage (Christoffersen)
Null-Hypothesis:    Correct Exceedances and
                Independence of Failures
LR.cc Statistic:    1.131
LR.cc Critical:        9.21
LR.cc p-value:        0.568
Reject Null:        O
```

Kupiec's unconditional coverage compares the number of expected versus actual exceedances given the tail probability of VaR, while the Christoffersen test is a joint test of the unconditional coverage and the independence of the exceedances. In our case, despite the actual five exceedances versus an expectation of three, we can't reject the null hypothesis that the exceedances are correct and independent.

A plot of the backtesting performance can also be generated easily. First, create a zoo object using the extracted forecasted VaR from the ugarchroll object.

```
> intc_VaR <- zoo(intc_garch11_roll@forecast$VaR[, 1])
```

We overwrite the index property of the zoo object with rownames (year and month) from this object as well.

```
> index(intc_VaR) <- as.yearmon(rownames(intc_garch11_roll@forecast$VaR))
```

We do the same for the actual returns that are also stored in the ugarchroll object.

```
> intc_actual <- zoo(intc_garch11_roll@forecast$VaR[, 2])
> index(intc_actual) <-
as.yearmon(rownames(intc_garch11_roll@forecast$VaR))
```

Now, we are able to plot the VaR versus the actual returns of Intel using the following commands:

```
> plot(intc_actual, type = "b", main = "99% 1 Month VaR Backtesting",
+    xlab = "Date", ylab = "Return/VaR in percent")
> lines(intc_VaR, col = "red")
> legend("topright", inset=.05, c("Intel return","VaR"), col =
c("black","red"), lty = c(1,1))
```

The following figure shows the output of the preceding command lines:

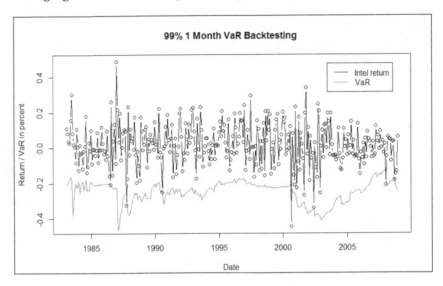

## Forecasting

Now that we can be reasonably sure that our risk model works properly, we can produce VaR forecasts as well. The function ugarchforecast takes as arguments the fitted GARCH model (intc_garch11_fit) and the number of periods for which a forecast should be produced (n.ahead = 12; that is, twelve months).

```
> intc_garch11_fcst <- ugarchforecast(intc_garch11_fit, n.ahead = 12)
```

The resulting forecast can be expected by querying the forecast object as shown in the following command lines:

```
> intc_garch11_fcst
*-----------------------------------*
*         GARCH Model Forecast       *
*-----------------------------------*
Model: sGARCH
Horizon: 12
Roll Steps: 0
Out of Sample: 0

0-roll forecast [T0=Dec 2008]:
      Series  Sigma
T+1   0.01911 0.1168
T+2   0.01911 0.1172
T+3   0.01911 0.1177
```

```
T+4   0.01911 0.1181
T+5   0.01911 0.1184
T+6   0.01911 0.1188
T+7   0.01911 0.1191
T+8   0.01911 0.1194
T+9   0.01911 0.1197
T+10  0.01911 0.1200
T+11  0.01911 0.1202
T+12  0.01911 0.1204
```

The one-period ahead forecast for the volatility (sigma) is 0.1168. Since we assume a normal distribution, the 99% VaR can be calculated using the 99% quantile (type in `qnorm(0.99)`) of the standard normal distribution. The one-month 99% VaR estimate for the next period is hence `qnorm(0.99)*0.1168 = 0.2717`. Hence, with 99% probability the monthly return is above -27%.

# Summary

In this chapter, we have applied R to selected problems in time series analysis. We covered the different ways of representing time series data, used an ARMA model to forecast house prices, improved our basic minimum variance hedge ratio using a cointegration relationship, and employed a GARCH model for risk management purposes. In the next chapter, you'll learn how you can use R for constructing an optimal portfolio.

# 2
# Portfolio Optimization

By now we are familiar with the basics of the **R** language. We know how to analyze data, call its built-in functions, and apply them to the selected problems in a time series analysis. In this chapter we will use and extend this knowledge to discuss an important practical application: portfolio optimization, or in other words, security selection. This section covers the idea behind portfolio optimization: the mathematical models and theoretical solutions. To improve programming skills, we will implement an algorithm line by line using real data to solve a real-world example. We will also use the pre-written R packages on the same data set.

Imagine that we live in a tropical island and have only USD 100 to invest. Investment possibilities on the island are very limited; we can invest our entire fund into either ice creams or umbrellas. The payoffs that depend on the weather are as follows:

| weather | ice cream | umbrella |
|---------|-----------|----------|
| sunny   | 120       | 90       |
| rainy   | 90        | 120      |

Suppose the probability of the weather being rainy or sunny is the same. If we cannot foresee or change the weather, the two options are clearly equivalent and we have an expected return of 5% [(0.5×120+0.5×90)/100-1=0.05] by investing in any of them.

What if we can split our funds between ice creams and umbrellas? Then we should invest USD 50 in both the options. This portfolio is riskless because whatever happens, we earn USD 45 with one asset and USD 60 with the other one. The expected return is still 5%, but now it is guaranteed since (45+60)/100-1=0.05.

The main concept of portfolio optimization (which won the Nobel Prize for Harry Markowitz in 1990) is captured in this example. Based on the correlation between investment products, we can reduce the risk (which in this case is measured by variance) of the portfolio and still get the desired expected return.

To be mathematically more precise, let $X$ and $Y$ be the random variables with the finite variances $\sigma_x^2$ and $\sigma_y^2$. The variance of their convex or affine combination is shown in the following quadratic function:

$$f(\alpha) = \operatorname{Var}(\alpha X + (1-\alpha)Y) = \alpha^2 \sigma_x^2 + (1-\alpha)^2 \sigma_y^2 + 2\alpha(1-\alpha)\operatorname{Cov}(X,Y)$$

For different values of their correlation, this quadratic function looks like the following diagram:

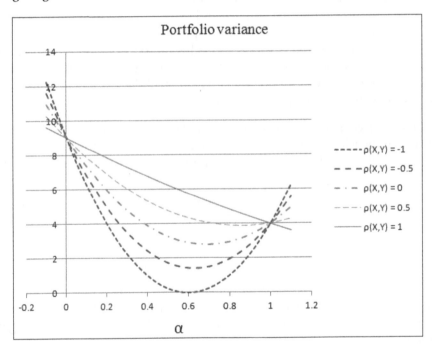

The variance (as a measure of risk) can completely be eliminated if and only if the correlation between $X$ and $Y$ is -1 or +1, and the variance of $X$ and $Y$ are not the same. Otherwise, the variance of the portfolio with optimal weights depends (in an absolutely non-trivial way) on all the three parameters ($\sigma_x^2$, $\sigma_y^2$, and $\operatorname{Cov}(X,Y)$), as we will see later in the *Theorem (Lagrange)* section.

# Mean-Variance model

The Mean-Variance model by Markowitz (*Markowitz, H.M. (March 1952)*) is practically the ice-cream/umbrella business in higher dimensions. For the mathematical formulation, we need some definitions.

They are explained as follows:

- By asset $X_i$, we mean a random variable with finite variance.
- By portfolio, we mean the combination of assets: $P = \sum w_i X_i$, where $\sum w_i = w\vec{1} = 1$, and $\vec{1} = (1,1...1)$. The combination can be affine or convex. In the affine case, there is no extra restriction on the weights. In the convex case, all the weights are non-negative.

- By optimization, we mean a process of choosing the best $w_i$ coefficients (weights) so that our portfolio meets our needs (that is, it has a minimal risk on the given expected return or has the highest expected return on a given level of risk, and so on).

Let $X_1, X_2,...X_n$ be the random return variables with a finite variance, $Q \in \mathbb{R}^{n \times n}$ be their covariance matrix, $r = (EX_1, EX_2,...EX_n)$ and $wr = \sum w_i r_i$.

We will focus on the following optimization problems:

- $\min\{w^T Q w \mid w \in \mathbb{R}^n, w\vec{1} = 1\}$          (1)
- $\max\{wr \mid w \in \mathbb{R}^n, w^T Q w = \sigma^2, w\vec{1} = 1\}$      (2)
- $\min\{w^T Q w \mid w \in \mathbb{R}^n, w\vec{1} = 1, wr = \mu\}$      (3)
- $\max\{wr - \lambda w^T Q w \mid w \in \mathbb{R}^n, w\vec{1} = 1\}$      (4)
- $\min\{\sigma^2(w^T X - Y) \mid w \in \mathbb{R}^n, w\vec{1} = 1\}$      (5)

It is clear that $w^T Q w$ is the variance of the portfolio and $wr$ is the expected return. For the sum of the weights we have $\vec{1}w = 1$, which means that we would like to invest 1 unit of cash. (We can also consider adding the $w \geq 0$ condition, which means that short selling is not allowed.) The problems are explained in detail in the following points:

- The first problem is to find the portfolio with a minimal risk. It can be nontrivial if there is no riskless asset.

- The second one is to maximize the expected return on a given level of variance.

- A slightly different approach is to find a portfolio with minimal variance on a desired level of expected return.

- The fourth problem is to maximize a simple utility function $\text{return} - \lambda * \text{risk}$, where $\lambda$ is the coefficient of risk tolerance; it's an arbitrary number that expresses our attitude to a risk. It is practically the same as the first problem.

- In the fifth problem, $Y$ is an $n+1$th asset (for example, an index), which we cannot purchase or don't want to purchase, but want to replicate it. Other similar problems can be formulated in the same way.
  It is clear that the second problem is a linear optimization with a quadratic constraint; all the others are quadratic functions with linear constraints. As we will see later, this is an important difference because linear constraints can be handled easily while quadratic constraints are more difficult to handle. In the next two sections, we will focus on the complexity and possible solutions of these problems.

# Solution concepts

In the last 50 years, many great algorithms have been developed for numerical optimization and these algorithms work well, especially in case of quadratic functions. As we have seen in the previous section, we only have quadratic functions and constraints; so these methods (that are implemented in R as well) can be used in the worst case scenarios (if there is nothing better).

However, a detailed discussion of numerical optimization is out of the scope of this book. Fortunately, in the special case of linear and quadratic functions and constraints, these methods are unnecessary; we can use the Lagrange theorem from the 18th century.

# Theorem (Lagrange)

If $f : \mathbb{R}^n \to \mathbb{R}$ and $g = (g_1, g_2, \ldots g_m) : \mathbb{R}^n \to \mathbb{R}^m$, (where $m < n$) have continuous partial derivatives and $a \in \{g(x) = 0\}$ is a relative extreme point of $f(x)$ subject to the $g(x) = 0$, constraint where $rank(g'(a)) = m$.

Then, there exist the coefficients $\lambda_1, \lambda_2, \ldots \lambda_m$ such that $f'(a) + \sum \lambda_i g_i'(a) = 0$.

In other words, all of the partial derivatives of the function $L := f - \sum \lambda_i g_i : \mathbb{R}^{m+n} \to \mathbb{R}$ are 0 (*Bertsekas Dimitri P. (1999)*).

In our case, the condition is also sufficient. The partial derivative of a quadratic function is linear, so the optimization leads to the problem of solving a linear system of equations, which is a high school task (unlike numerical methods).

Let's see, how this can be used to solve the third problem:

$$\min\{w^T Q w \mid w \in \mathbb{R}^n, w\vec{1} = 1, \quad wr = \mu\}$$

It can be shown that this problem is equivalent to the following system of linear equations:

$$\begin{bmatrix} Q & \vec{1} & \vec{r} \\ \vec{1} & 0 & 0 \\ \vec{r} & 0 & 0 \end{bmatrix} \begin{bmatrix} w \\ \lambda_1 \\ \lambda_2 \end{bmatrix} = \begin{bmatrix} 0 \\ 1 \\ \mu \end{bmatrix}$$

(Two rows and two columns are added to the covariance matrix, so we have conditions to determine the two Lagrange multipliers as well.) We can expect a unique solution for this system.

It is worth emphasizing that what we get with the Lagrange theorem is not an optimization problem anymore. Just as in one dimension, minimizing a quadratic function leads to taking a derivative and a linear system of equations, which is trivial from the point of complexity. Now let's see what to do with the return maximization problem:

$$\max\{wr \mid w \in \mathbb{R}^n, w^T Q w = \sigma, w\vec{1} = 1\}$$

It's easy to see that the derivative of the Lagrange function subject to $\lambda$ is the constraint itself.

To see this, take the derivative of $L$:

- $L := f + \sum \lambda_i g_i$
- $\partial L / \partial \lambda_i = g_i$

So this leads to non-linear equations, which is more of an art than a science.

# Working with real data

It is useful to know that portfolio optimization is totally integrated in various R packages that we will discuss later. However, it's better to walk before we run; so let's start with a simple self-made R function that we would also itemize line by line as follows:

```
minvariance <- function(assets, mu = 0.005) {
    return  <- log(tail(assets, -1) / head(assets, -1))
    Q       <- rbind(cov(return), rep(1, ncol(assets)),
                colMeans(return))
    Q       <- cbind(Q, rbind(t(tail(Q, 2)), matrix(0, 2, 2)))
    b       <- c(rep(0, ncol(assets)), 1, mu)
    solve(Q, b)
}
```

This is a direct implementation of the algorithm that we discussed in the *Theorem (Lagrange)* section.

For demonstration purposes, we have fetched some IT stock prices from a **Quandl** superset (http://www.quandl.com/USER_1KR/1KT), which is a public service providing an easy access to a large amount of quant data. Although the URL points to a downloadable comma-separated values (CSV) file (http://www.quandl.com/api/v1/datasets/USER_1KR/1KT.csv) that can be saved to a disk and imported to R with read.csv, there is a more intuitive way to do so with the help of the keys included in the previous URLs:

```
> library(Quandl)
> IT <- Quandl('USER_1KR/1KT',
+           start_date = '2008-01-01', end_date = '2012-12-31')
Warning message:
In Quandl("USER_1KR/1KT", start_date = "2008-01-01", end_date = "2012-12-
31"):
```

The preceding warning message would appear if you are not using an authentication token. Please visit http://www.quandl.com/help/r or you may download only 10 datasets a day from Quandl.

```
> str(IT)
'data.frame':  1259 obs. of  6 variables:
 $ Date: Date, format: "2008-01-02" "2008-01-03" ...
 $ AAPL: num  199 195 191 181 180 ...
 $ GOOG: num  693 685 680 654 653 ...
 $ MSFT: num  35.8 35.2 35.2 34.5 34.7 ...
 $ IBM : num  109 105 104 100 100 ...
 $ T   : num  41.5 41.2 41 41.1 41.3 ...
```

So, we loaded the Quandl package that provides the `Quandl` function taking several arguments:

- The first parameter (code="USER_1KR/1KT") is the dataset code on Quandl
- The `start_date` and `end_date` parameters optionally specify the time period we are interested in and that is set to be the last 5 years from now
- Please see `?Quandl` for more options; for example, `type` could be used to import the data that already exists in some time-series object instead of a raw `data.frame`

The `str` command run on the newly created `IT` variable shows the internal structure of the R object, which currently holds a `Date` field and the prices of five assets in a numeric format.

After assigning the prices from `IT` (without the first `Date` column) to `assets`, let us run the preceding `minvariance` function's body line by line. First, we compute the return of the assets by dividing each but the first value (`tail`) with the preceding (`head`) and computing `log` for each quotient:

```
> assets <- IT[, -1]
> return <- log(tail(assets, -1) / head(assets, -1))
```

Please note that the return can be also computed with the `returns` function from the **timeSeries** package that we did not call here for didactical purposes. To verify what our command did, let us check the first few values of the newly created variable:

```
> head(return)
          AAPL          GOOG          MSFT           IBM             T
2 -0.019560774 -0.011044063 -0.0160544217 -0.038916144 -0.0072534167
3 -0.020473237 -0.008161516 -0.0008521517 -0.008429976 -0.0043774389
4 -0.054749384 -0.038621208 -0.0183544011 -0.036242948  0.0007309051
5 -0.006142967 -0.001438475  0.0046202797 -0.001997005  0.0051014322
6 -0.050317921 -0.035793820 -0.0396702524 -0.023154566 -0.0514590970
7  0.036004806  0.023482511  0.0292444412 -0.003791959 -0.0123204844
```

Next, we start building the left side of the linear equality system specified at the

Lagrange theorem: $\begin{bmatrix} Q \\ 1 \\ r \end{bmatrix}$ where we combine the covariance matrix (cov), ones repeated (rep) by the number of columns (ncol) in the dataset and the means (colMeans) of the returns as rows (rbind).

```
> Q <- rbind(cov(return), rep(1, ncol(assets)), colMeans(return))
```

That would end up as follows:

```
> round(Q, 5)
          AAPL     GOOG      MSFT      IBM        T
AAPL  0.00063  0.00034   0.00025  0.00023  0.00022
GOOG  0.00034  0.00046   0.00023  0.00019  0.00018
MSFT  0.00025  0.00023   0.00034  0.00018  0.00018
IBM   0.00023  0.00019   0.00018  0.00024  0.00016
T     0.00022  0.00018   0.00018  0.00016  0.00028
      1.00000  1.00000   1.00000  1.00000  1.00000
      0.00075  0.00001  -0.00024  0.00044 -0.00018
```

Please note that we have rounded the results to five digits for the sake of readability. Also note that the average return of the Microsoft (MSFT) and AT&T was negative. Now, we also combine the last two rows of the matrix (tail) as new columns (rbind) on the left to make it complete for the linear system with the extra zeros specified in the Lagrange theorem (matrix of 2x2):

```
> Q <- cbind(Q, rbind(t(tail(Q, 2)), matrix(0, 2, 2)))
> round(Q, 5)
          AAPL     GOOG      MSFT      IBM        T
AAPL  0.00063  0.00034   0.00025  0.00023  0.00022  1  0.00075
GOOG  0.00034  0.00046   0.00023  0.00019  0.00018  1  0.00001
MSFT  0.00025  0.00023   0.00034  0.00018  0.00018  1 -0.00024
IBM   0.00023  0.00019   0.00018  0.00024  0.00016  1  0.00044
T     0.00022  0.00018   0.00018  0.00016  0.00028  1 -0.00018
      1.00000  1.00000   1.00000  1.00000  1.00000  0  0.00000
      0.00075  0.00001  -0.00024  0.00044 -0.00018  0  0.00000
```

By default, mu is 0.005 (specified in the minvariance function's argument); this is the last value of the vector on the right side of the linear system $\begin{bmatrix} 0 \\ 1 \\ \mu \end{bmatrix}$:

```
> mu <- 0.005
> b   <- c(rep(0, ncol(assets)), 1, mu)
> b
[1] 0.000 0.000 0.000 0.000 0.000 1.000 0.005
```

After successfully building the parts of the linear equality system, you are only left with the task of solving it:

```
> solve(Q, b)
          AAPL           GOOG           MSFT            IBM              T
  2.3130600636 -1.0928257246 -2.7830264740   4.9871895547 -2.4243974197
-0.0001254637 -1.2082468413
```

The preceding code is equivalent to running the function in one go, which would take the dataset and optionally, the desired return as its arguments. The result is the vector of optimal weights and the Lagrange multipliers to get the desired expected return with a minimal variance:

```
> minvariance(IT[, -1])
          AAPL           GOOG           MSFT            IBM              T
  2.3130600636 -1.0928257246 -2.7830264740   4.9871895547 -2.4243974197
-0.0001254637 -1.2082468413
```

Note that on top of the Microsoft and AT&T stocks, Google is also shorted in the optimum. We can use this output to get a complete solution for the optimization problem, which can be also processed further with other software with the help of the `write.csv` function. And instead of calculating the minimum variance for a given level of return, we can also get the minimum variance for a larger range of returns. If we modify the code, we can get something as follows:

```
frontier <- function(assets) {
    return <- log(tail(assets, -1) / head(assets, -1))
    Q   <- cov(return)
    n   <- ncol(assets)
    r   <- colMeans(return)
    Q1 <- rbind(Q, rep(1, n), r)
    Q1 <- cbind(Q1, rbind(t(tail(Q1, 2)), matrix(0, 2, 2)))
    rbase <- seq(min(r), max(r), length = 100)
    s   <- sapply(rbase, function(x) {
```

```
            y <- head(solve(Q1, c(rep(0, n), 1, x)), n)
            y %*% Q %*% y
    })
    plot(s, rbase, xlab = 'Return', ylab = 'Variance')
}
```

The code is the same, except that it takes a number (length = 100) of different return values between (seq) the minimum and maximum asset returns and calculates the variance of the optimal portfolios. We can then plot the return-variance pairs (s and rbase) to illustrate the solution of the problem. The result is shown in the following screenshot:

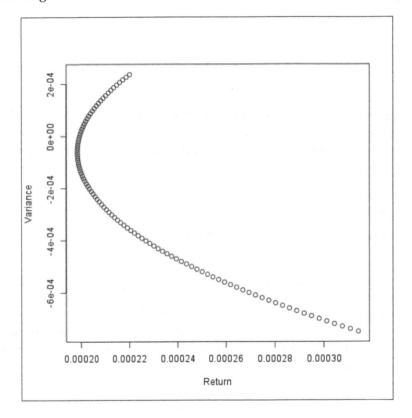

On the variance-return plane, the desired return-minimum variance curve is called **Portfolio Frontier**. Ignoring its downward sloping part (the same variance can be reached with a higher return), we get **Efficient Frontier**; there is no reason to choose a portfolio outside Efficient Frontier.

It is well-known that it is enough to calculate Portfolio Frontier for two given levels of return and combine the resulting portfolios to get the whole frontier.

Similar results can be achieved with some built-in functions of R packages without much coding. For example, the **fPortfolio** package provides a bunch of useful methods, ready to be applied on time-series objects. For this end, we have to transform the asset columns of the original `IT` dataset to a `timeSeries` object defined by the first column:

```
> library(timeSeries)
> IT <- timeSeries(IT[, 2:6], IT[, 1])
```

Just like we did in the mean-variance function, the return can be defined in the time-series by dividing each element with the prior one and computing the logarithm, although some useful time-series commands (such as `lag`) can make this easier:

```
> log(lag(IT) / IT)
```

Or even simpler with the other built-in functions:

```
> IT_return <- returns(IT)
```

As we have a time-series object now, it is extremely easy to plot the returns:

```
> chart.CumReturns(IT_return, legend.loc = 'topleft', main = '')
```

The return of the five stocks in `IT_return` would then look like the following figure:

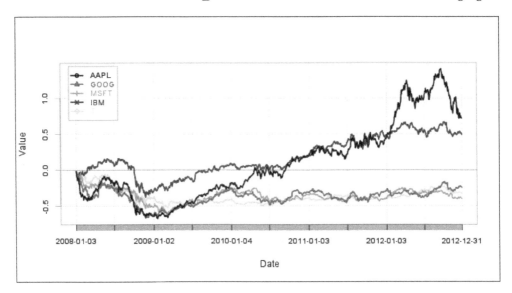

The preceding frontier chart can be interactively drawn by plotting the results of `portfolioFrontier`:

```
> library(fPortfolio)
> plot(portfolioFrontier(IT_return))


Make a plot selection (or 0 to exit):


1:    Plot Efficient Frontier
2:    Add Minimum Risk Portfolio
3:    Add Tangency Portfolio
4:    Add Risk/Return of Single Assets
5:    Add Equal Weights Portfolio
6:    Add Two Asset Frontiers [LongOnly Only]
7:    Add Monte Carlo Portfolios
8:    Add Sharpe Ratio [Markowitz PF Only]
```

To mimic what we have implemented in the preceding code, let us render the Frontier plot of short sale constraints:

```
> Spec = portfolioSpec()
> setSolver(Spec) = "solveRshortExact"
> Frontier <- portfolioFrontier(as.timeSeries(IT_return),
+                 Spec, > constraints = "Short")
> frontierPlot(Frontier, col = rep('orange', 2), pch = 19)
> monteCarloPoints(Frontier, mcSteps = 1000, cex = 0.25, pch = 19)
> grid()
```

In the preceding code, we have set a special `portfolioSpec` S4 object with a function (`solveRshortExact`) that optimizes an unlimited short selling portfolio. The result of the computation (`portfolioFrontier`) is rendered by `frontierPlot` with orange colored circles (`pch = 19`); some smaller (`cex = 0.25`) Monte Carlo-simulated points are also added to the graph beside a grid in the background as shown in the following diagram:

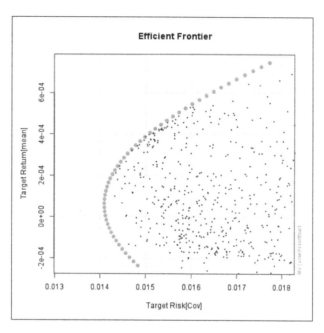

# Tangency portfolio and Capital Market Line

What happens when a riskless asset $R$ is added to the model? If $\sigma_R = 0$ and $X$ is any risky portfolio, then $Var(\alpha R + (1-\alpha)X) = (1-\alpha)^2 Var(X)$ and obviously, $E(\alpha R + (1-\alpha)X) = \alpha E(R) + (1-\alpha)E(X)$. This means that those portfolios form a straight line on the mean-standard deviation plane. Any portfolio on this line is available by investing into R and X. It is clear that the best choice for $X$ is the point where this line is tangent to Efficient Frontier. This tangency point is called the market portfolio or tangency portfolio, and the tangent of Efficient Frontier of risky assets at this point is called Capital Market Line (CML), which consists of the efficient portfolios of all the assets in this case. The last question that we address regarding the mean-variance model is how the market portfolio (or equivalently, the CML) can be determined.

We can easily modify the variance minimization code to accomplish this. First of all, if we add a riskless asset, a full-zero row and column is added to the covariance matrix (where n is the number of assets including the riskless one):

```
> n <- 6; mu <- 0.005
> Q <- cbind(cov(return), rep(0, n - 1))
> Q <- rbind(Q, rep(0, n))
```

And the riskless return (let rf be 0.0001) is added to the return vector:

```
> r <- c(colMeans(return), rf)
```

After this, we can use the new covariance matrix and the new return vector to determine the optimal portfolio weights and then eliminate the *n*th asset based on the minvariance code described in the *Working with real data* section:

```
> Q <- rbind(Q, rep(1, n), r)
> Q <- cbind(Q, rbind(t(tail(Q, 2)), matrix(0, 2, 2)))
> b <- c(rep(0, n), 1, mu)
```

With the following intermediate results:

```
> round(Q, 6)
```

|      | AAPL     | GOOG     | MSFT     | IBM      | T        |       |   | r         |
|------|----------|----------|----------|----------|----------|-------|---|-----------|
| AAPL | 0.000630 | 0.000338 | 0.000249 | 0.000233 | 0.000218 | 0e+00 | 1 | 0.000748  |
| GOOG | 0.000338 | 0.000462 | 0.000226 | 0.000186 | 0.000182 | 0e+00 | 1 | 0.000008  |
| MSFT | 0.000249 | 0.000226 | 0.000341 | 0.000178 | 0.000177 | 0e+00 | 1 | -0.000236 |
| IBM  | 0.000233 | 0.000186 | 0.000178 | 0.000240 | 0.000157 | 0e+00 | 1 | 0.000439  |
| T    | 0.000218 | 0.000182 | 0.000177 | 0.000157 | 0.000283 | 0e+00 | 1 | -0.000179 |
|      | 0.000000 | 0.000000 | 0.000000 | 0.000000 | 0.000000 | 0e+00 | 1 | 0.000100  |
|      | 1.000000 | 1.000000 | 1.000000 | 1.000000 | 1.000000 | 1e+00 | 0 | 0.000000  |
| r    | 0.000748 | 0.000008 | -0.000236 | 0.000439 | -0.000179 | 1e-04 | 0 | 0.000000  |

```
> b
[1] 0.000 0.000 0.000 0.000 0.000 0.000 1.000 0.005
```

After solving the equation, the result is the market portfolio:

```
> w <- solve(Q, b)
> w <- head(w, -3)
> w / sum(w)
       AAPL        GOOG        MSFT         IBM           T
 -10.154891    4.990912   12.347784  -18.010579   11.826774
```

# Noise in the covariance matrix

When we optimize a portfolio, we don't have the real covariance matrix and the expected return vector (that are the inputs of the mean-variance model); we use observations to estimate them, so Q, r, and the output of the model are also random variables.

Without going into the details, we can say that this leads to surprisingly great uncertainty in the model. In spite of the strong law of large numbers, optimal portfolio weights sometimes vary between ±200%. Fortunately, if we have a few years' data (daily returns), the relative error of the measured risk is only 20-25 %.

# When variance is not enough

Variance as a risk measure is convenient, but has some drawbacks. For instance, when using variance, positive changes in the return can be considered as the increase of risk. Therefore, more sophisticated risk measures have been developed.

For example, see the following short demo about various methods applied against the previously described IT_return assets for a quick overview about the options provided by the fPortfolio package:

```
> Spec <- portfolioSpec()
> setSolver(Spec) <- "solveRshortExact"
> setTargetReturn(Spec) <- mean(colMeans(IT_return))
> efficientPortfolio(IT_return, Spec, 'Short')
> minvariancePortfolio(IT_return, Spec, 'Short')
> minriskPortfolio(IT_return, Spec)
> maxreturnPortfolio(IT_return, Spec)
```

These R expressions return different portfolio weights computed by various methods not discussed in this introductory chapter. Please refer to the package bundled documentation, such as ?portfolio, and the relevant articles and book chapters in the *References* section for details.

# Summary

This chapter covered portfolio optimization. After presenting the main idea, we introduced the Markowitz model and its mathematical formulation. We discussed the methods for possible solutions and implemented a simple algorithm to demonstrate how these methods work on real data. We have also used pre-written R packages to solve the same problem. We broadly discussed other important subjects like the market portfolio, the uncertainty in the estimation of the covariance matrix, and the risk measures beyond variance. We hope that this was a useful first run on the topic and you are encouraged to study it further or check out the next chapter, which is about a related subject—asset pricing models.

# 3
# Asset Pricing Models

Covered in this chapter are the problem of absolute pricing (*Cochrane 2005*) and how the value of assets with uncertain payments is determined based on their risk. *Chapter 2, Portfolio Optimization*, modeled the decision-making of an individual investor based on the analysis of the assets' return in a mean variance framework. This chapter focuses on whether or not equilibrium can exist in financial markets, what conditions are needed, and how it can be characterized. Two main approaches — **Capital Asset Pricing Model** and **Arbitrage Pricing Theory** — will be presented, which use completely different assumptions and argumentation, but give similar descriptions of the return evolution.

According to the concept of **relative pricing**, the riskiness of the underlying product is already involved in its price and, so, it does not play any further role in the pricing of the derived instrument; this will be presented in *Chapter 6, Derivatives Pricing*. The no-arbitrage argument will force consistency in the prices of the derivative and underlying assets there.

The objective of this chapter is to present the relationship between the asset return and the risk factor. We will explain how to download and clean data from multiple sources. **Linear regression** is used to measure the dependence and the connected **hypothesis test** shows the significance of the results. The one-factor index model is tested through a two-step regression process and the financial interpretation of the results is shown.

# Capital Asset Pricing Model

The first type of model explaining asset prices uses economic considerations. Using the results of the portfolio selection presented in the previous chapter, the **Capital Asset Pricing Model (CAPM)** gives an answer to the question asking what can be said of the market by aggregating the rational investors' decisions and, also, by what assumption the equilibrium would evolve. *Sharpe (1964)* and *Lintner (1965)* prove the existence of the equilibrium subject to the following assumptions:

- Individual investors are price takers
- Single-period investment horizon
- Investments are limited to traded financial assets
- No taxes and no transaction costs
- Information is costless and available to all investors
- Investors are rational mean-variance optimizers
- Homogenous expectations

In a world where these assumptions are held, all investors will hold the same portfolio of risky assets, which is the market portfolio. The market portfolio contains all securities and the proportion of each security is its market value as a percentage of the total market value. The risk premium on the market depends on the average risk aversion of all market participants. The best-known consequence of the resulting equilibrium is a linear relationship between market risk premium and the individual security's risk:

$$E(r_i) - r_f = \beta_i \left[ E(r_m) - r_f \right] \qquad (1)$$

$E(r_i)$ is the expected return of a certain security, $r_f$ is the risk-free return, $E(r_m)$ is the expected return of the market portfolio. The risk in CAPM is measured by the beta $\beta_i$, which is a function of the individual security's covariance with the market and the variance of the market return:

$$\beta_i = \frac{Cov_{i,m}}{Var_m} \qquad (2)$$

$Cov_{i,m}$ is the covariance between the given security's return and the market return, while $Var_m$ is the variance of the market return.

Beta has numerous interpretations. On the one hand, beta shows the sensitivity of a stock's return to the return of the market portfolio and, on the other, a certain security's beta shows how much risk that security adds to the market portfolio. The CAPM states that the market gives a higher return only in cases of higher systematic risk since unsystematic risk can be diversified, so no risk premium can be paid after that.

If we rearrange equation **(1)**, we will get a linear equation of the so called **Security Market Line (SML)**:

$$E(r_i) = r_f + \beta_i \left[ E(r_m) - r_f \right] \qquad (3)$$

CAPM states that in equilibrium, every security should be on the SML; so, this equation holds for each security or portfolio even if they are not efficient. If this equation is not fulfilled, there is a lack of equilibrium on the market. For example, if a security's return on the market is higher than it should be according to the CAPM, every investor has to change the composition of his/her portfolio in order to decrease the security's return and fulfill the above equation.

# Arbitrage Pricing Theory

The **Arbitrage Pricing Theory (APT)** of *Ross (1977)* is also used in finance to determine the return of different securities. The APT states that, in equilibrium, no arbitrage opportunity can exist and, also, that the expected return of an asset is the linear combination of multiple random factors (*Wilmott 2007*). These factors can be various macro-economic factors or market indices. In this model, each factor has a specific beta coefficient:

$$r_i = \alpha_i + \sum_{j=1}^{n} \beta_{ij} F_j + e_i \qquad (4)$$

$\alpha_i$ is a constant denoting security i; $\beta_{ij}$ is the sensitivity of security i to factor j; $F_j$ is the systematic factor; while $e_i$ is the security's unsystematic risk, with zero mean.

A central notion of the APT is the **factorportfolio**. A factorportfolio is a well-diversified portfolio which reacts to only one of the factors, so it has zero beta for all other factors, and a beta of 1 to that specified factor. Assuming the existence of the factorportfolios, it can be shown using the arbitrage argument that any well-diversified portfolio's risk premium is equal to the weighted sum of the factorportfolios' risk premium (*Medvegyev-Száz 2010*). If it is to hold for every well-diversified portfolio, the expected return of an individual security will be built up by the risk premium of the factor ($RP_j$) and its sensitivity to the factor ($\beta_{ij}$):

$$E(r_i) = r_f + \sum_{j=1}^{n} \beta_{ij} RP_j \qquad (5)$$

In case there is only one factor in the APT model, which is the return of the market portfolio, we call the model the index model. Moreover, if $\alpha_i$ is zero, we will get the exact pricing formula of CAPM.

The differences between the CAPM and APT are as follows:

- CAPM is an equilibrium model, building on economic considerations, while APT is a statistical model, using arbitrage arguments.

- In the case of APT, an expected return-beta relation can be given if one has a well-diversified portfolio so that this can be constructed in practice by having a large number of assets in the portfolio. While, in the case of CAPM, the so-called market portfolio cannot be constructed.

- CAPM states that the expected return-beta relation holds for every security, while APT states that this is for almost every security.

- When there is mispricing on the market, in the case of APT, it is enough if only a few investors change the portfolio structure to get the fair price of a security; while, in the case of CAPM, every investor has to do so.

# Beta estimation

The sensitivity of a security towards a factor can be estimated from past price movements. We will estimate the beta from the one-factor index model. First, we show the process of collecting and synchronizing data from different sources and then present the simple beta estimation method and, at last, a linear regression model is built.

# Data selection

We download the time series of the price of a given stock, for example Google, and the time series of the price of the market index, the S&P 500, from June 1st 2009 to June 1st 2013 from Quandl, as discussed in the second chapter:

```
> library(Quandl)
> Quandl.auth("yourauthenticationtoken")
> G <- Quandl('GOOG/NASDAQ_GOOG',
+    start_date = '2009-06-01', end_date = '2013-06-01')
```

The resulting `G` is a variable containing 6 variables, from which we only need the `Close` values:

```
> str(G)
'data.frame':      1018 obs. of  6 variables:
 $ Date  : Date, format: "2009-06-01" "2009-06-02" ...
 $ Open  : num  419 426 426 435 445 ...
 $ High  : num  430 430 432 441 447 ...
 $ Low   : num  419 423 424 434 439 ...
 $ Close : num  427 428 432 440 444 ...
 $ Volume: num  3323431 2626012 3535593 3639434 3681002 ...
> G <- G$Close
```

The same code is run for the S&P 500 data, although we deal with the `Adjusted Close` values now:

```
> SP500 <- Quandl('YAHOO/INDEX_GSPC',
+    start_date = '2009-06-01', end_date = '2013-06-01')
> SP500 <- SP500$'Adjusted Close'
```

Adjusted closing prices are used as they have been corrected with dividends and splits. As Google paid no dividend and had no split in the period, such adjustment is unnecessary in this example. We will also need the time series of the risk-free return, which will be the 1 month USD LIBOR rate. Although we will be working with daily returns, the 1 month rates can be regarded as short-term rates and are less affected by random noises than the overnight rates.

```
> LIBOR <- Quandl('FED/RILSPDEPM01_N_B',
+    start_date = '2009-06-01', end_date = '2013-06-01')
> LIBOR <- LIBOR$Value
```

As you can see from the previous Quandl calls, each time, the series was fetched from different data providers. This also results in some differences in the data structure as we have `Close` values with Google, `Adjusted Close` values with S&P 500, and simply `Values` for the `LIBOR` data. The length of the vectors does not seem to be equal either:

```
> sapply(list(G, SP500, LIBOR), length)
[1] 1018 1008 1024
```

This means that some time series also include dates that are omitted from the others. Let us define the `intersect` function of the dates and filter the results to only those cells after re-downloading the values:

```
> G      <- Quandl('GOOG/NASDAQ_GOOG',
+           start_date = '2009-06-01', end_date = '2013-06-01')
> SP500 <- Quandl('YAHOO/INDEX_GSPC',
+           start_date = '2009-06-01', end_date = '2013-06-01')
> LIBOR <- Quandl('FED/RILSPDEPM01_N_B',
+           start_date = '2009-06-01', end_date = '2013-06-01')
```

As the `intersect` function can only be applied to two vectors, we call the `Reduce` function to identify the common dates in the three time series:

```
> cdates <- Reduce(intersect, list(G$Date, SP500$Date,LIBOR$Date))
```

Now, let us simply filter all three data frames to the relevant cells to get the vectors:

```
G      <- G[G$Date %in% cdates, 'Close']
SP500 <- SP500[SP500$Date %in% cdates, 'Adjusted Close']
LIBOR <- LIBOR[LIBOR$Date %in% cdates, 'Value']
```

After downloading and cleaning the data, you have to calculate the log-returns ($r_t$) of the stock and the market index using the following formula:

$$r_{it} = ln\left(\frac{s_t}{s_{t-1}}\right) \qquad (6)$$

$s_t$ is the market price on day `t`. In R, this would be expressed as a function (see *Chapter 2, Portfolio Optimization*, for details):

```
> logreturn <- function(x) log(tail(x, -1) / head(x, -1))
```

For the next step, the risk premiums should be determined by subtracting the risk-free daily log-return ($r_{ft}$). As the LIBOR rates are quoted on a money-market basis — actual/360 day-count convention — and the time series contains the rates in percentage, the following formula is to be used:

$$r_{ft} = ln\left(1 + \frac{USDLIBOR}{36000} * \left((t+1) - (t)\right)\right) \tag{7}$$

t and t-1 refer to the dates, so the difference is the number of days between the two closing values, that is usually 1, in our case, or more if there are non-working days in-between. The results can be computed in R easily using the following commands:

```
> rft <- log(1 + head(LIBOR, -1)/36000 * diff(cdates))
> str(rft)
num [1:1001] 1.81e-05 1.81e-05 1.81e-05 1.81e-05 5.42e-05 ...
```

We have computed (t+1) − t by computing the diff between the common dates, just described. And the risk premium ($R_{it}$) is given by:

$$R_{it} = r_{it} - r_{ft} \tag{8}$$

# Simple beta estimation

Once we have both time series; the individual asset's (Google, in our case) and the market's (S&P 500) risk premium, beta can be calculated based on equation **(2)**:

```
> cov(logreturn(G) - rft, logreturn(SP500) - rft) /
+    var(logreturn(SP500) - rft)
[1] 0.8997941
```

This could be also simplified by adding a new function to describe the risk premium:

```
> riskpremium <- function(x) logreturn(x) - rft
> cov(riskpremium(G), riskpremium(SP500)) / var(riskpremium(SP500))
[1] 0.8997941
```

This way of calculating beta differs from equation **(2)**, since we've used the risk premiums instead of the returns. As CAPM and APT are both one-period models, correction with the risk-free return on both sides does not affect the result. On the other hand, upon estimating beta from the time series, we have to decide whether to use returns or risk premiums in the model as the parameters will differ, except for in the case of a constant risk-free return (*Medvegyev-Száz 2010*). We follow the previously described method as we would follow the financial literature, but we have to add that Merryl Lynch calculates betas from returns.

# Beta estimation from linear regression

We can use linear regression in order to estimate beta, where the explanatory variable is the **Market Risk Premium** (**MRP**), while the dependent variable will be the risk premium of the security. So, the regression equation has the following form, which is the formula for the **Security Characteristic Line** (**SCL**):

$$R_i = \alpha_i + \beta_i R_m + e_i \qquad (9)$$

We will use the **Ordinary Least Squared** (**OLS**) estimation to determine the linear regression model of equation **(8)**. The intercept of the characteristic line is $\alpha$, the part of the stock return unexplained by the market factor. The slope of the function (equation **(8)**) shows the sensitivity toward the market factor, measured by beta.

We can easily compute the regression model using the built-in `lm` command in R:

```
> (fit <- lm(riskpremium(G) ~ riskpremium(SP500)))


Call:
lm(formula = riskpremium(G) ~ riskpremium(SP500))


Coefficients:
       (Intercept)   riskpremium(SP500)
         0.0002078            0.8997941
```

We have not only saved the results, but also printed them because of the extra braces we've added. With the help of the model, it is also easy to plot the characteristic line of Google on a chart that shows the risk premium of Google as a function of the market risk premium.

```
> plot(riskpremium(SP500), riskpremium(G))
> abline(fit, col = 'red')
```

The following figure shows the results. On the x axis there is the MRP, while the y axis shows the risk premium of the Google stock:

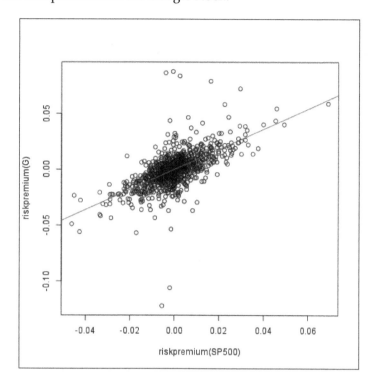

According to CAPM, $\alpha$ equals to zero, therefore we will assume $\alpha_i$ to be 0, then we release this restriction. We can force $\alpha$ to be zero by passing -1 in the model:

```
> fit <- lm(riskpremium(G) ~ -1 + riskpremium(SP500))
```

The summary of the results of the regression model in R are as follows:

```
> summary(fit)

Call:
lm(formula = riskpremium(G) ~ -1 + riskpremium(SP500))

Residuals:
     Min        1Q     Median        3Q        Max
-0.089794 -0.005553  0.000166  0.005520  0.117087
```

```
Coefficients:
                  Estimate Std. Error t value Pr(>|t|)
riskpremium(SP500)  0.90048    0.03501   25.72   <2e-16 ***
---
Signif. codes:  0 '***' 0.001 '**' 0.01 '*' 0.05 '.' 0.1 ' ' 1

Residual standard error: 0.0124 on 1000 degrees of freedom
Multiple R-squared:  0.3982,     Adjusted R-squared:  0.3976
F-statistic: 661.6 on 1 and 1000 DF,  p-value: < 2.2e-16
```

The high `F-statistic` value shows that the model has explaining power, beta proves to be significant, and the null-hypothesis—beta would be zero—is to be rejected at any significance level. These results are in line with CAPM.

If we're running the test by releasing the assumption of zero $\alpha$, we can see that the intercept does not differ significantly from zero. The high `p-value` value shows that we cannot reject the null-hypothesis at any usual (above 90%) significance level:

```
> summary(lm(riskpremium(G) ~ riskpremium(SP500)))


Call:
lm(formula = riskpremium(G) ~ riskpremium(SP500))


Residuals:
     Min        1Q    Median        3Q       Max
-0.089999 -0.005757 -0.000045  0.005307  0.116883


Coefficients:
                    Estimate Std. Error t value Pr(>|t|)
(Intercept)        0.0002078  0.0003924   0.529    0.597
riskpremium(SP500) 0.8997941  0.0350463  25.674   <2e-16 ***
---
Signif. codes:  0 '***' 0.001 '**' 0.01 '*' 0.05 '.' 0.1 ' ' 1

Residual standard error: 0.01241 on 999 degrees of freedom
Multiple R-squared:  0.3975,     Adjusted R-squared:  0.3969
F-statistic: 659.2 on 1 and 999 DF,  p-value: < 2.2e-16
```

We can check the residuals on a joint plot as shown in the following figure.

```
> par(mfrow = c(2, 2))
> plot(fit)
```

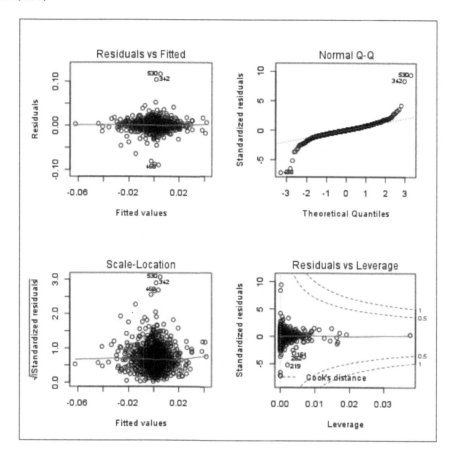

You can also find built-in functions in the **PerformanceAnalytics** package, `CAPM.alpha` and `CAPM.beta`, that calculate the parameters alpha and beta for a given asset. The requested parameters are the series of the asset's and the benchmark asset's return and the risk-free rate.

# Model testing

The first tests on the beta-return relationship used two-phase linear regression (*Lintner 1965*). The first regression estimates the security characteristic line and beta of the individual securities as described above. In the second regression, the security's risk premium is the dependent variable, whereas beta is the explanatory variable. The null-hypothesis assumes the intercept to be zero and the slope of the curve to be the market risk premium, which is estimated as the average of the sample. The test can be extended by an additional explanatory variable: the individual variance.

# Data collection

We will present the test using a sample of the US market in the pre-crisis period between 2003 and 2007. As daily data includes more short-term effects, we will apply the test on monthly returns calculated from the daily time series. So, we need the time series of the daily price of more stocks; let us download the prices of the first 100 stocks from S&P 500 in alphabetical order between 2003 and 2007:

```
> symbols <- c("A", "AA", "AAPL", "ABC", "ABT", "ACE", "ACN", "ACT",
"ADBE", "ADI", "ADM", "ADP", "ADSK", "AEE", "AEP", "AES","AET", "AFL",
"AGN", "AIG", "AIV", "AIZ", "AKAM", "ALL", "ALTR", "ALXN", "AMAT", "AMD",
"AMGN", "AMP", "AMT", "AMZN", "AN", "ANF", "AON", "APA", "APC", "APD",
"APH", "APOL", "ARG", "ATI", "AVB", "AVP", "AVY", "AXP", "AZO", "BA",
"BAC", "BAX", "BBBY", "BBT", "BBY", "BCR", "BDX", "BEAM", "BEN", "BF.B",
"BHI", "BIIB", "BK", "BLK", "BLL", "BMC", "BMS", "BMY", "BRCM", "BRK.B",
"BSX", "BTU", "BXP", "C", "CA", "CAG", "CAH", "CAM", "CAT", "CB", "CBG",
"CBS", "CCE", "CCI", "CCL", "CELG", "CERN", "CF", "CHK", "CHRW", "CI",
"CINF", "CL", "CLF", "CLX", "CMA", "CMCSA", "CME")
```

Please note that the previous list includes only 96 stock names as four stocks had too many missing values in the referenced time interval.

Let us download these datasets from a uniform database with the `tseries` package:

```
> library(tseries)
> res <- lapply(symbols, function(symbol)
+    get.hist.quote(symbol, quote = "AdjClose", quiet = TRUE,
+    start = as.Date('2003-01-01'), end = as.Date('2007-01-01')))
```

So, we call the `get.hist.quote` function to each `symbol` to download the Adjusted close data from the default (Yahoo!) provider without any details about the progress (`quiet`). Please note that the fetching process might take some time and will result in a list of 96 time series. Now, let us also update `SP500` and `LIBOR` for the new time interval and define the new intersect for the common dates:

```
> LIBOR <- Quandl('FED/RILSPDEPM01_N_B',
+           start_date = '2003-01-01', end_date = '2007-01-01')
> SP500 <- Quandl('YAHOO/INDEX_GSPC',
+           start_date = '2003-01-01', end_date = '2007-01-01')
> cdates <- intersect(LIBOR$Date, SP500$Date)
```

As explained above, we need a monthly dataset instead of the downloaded daily values; let us pick the first values in each month. To this end, we need to save the list of the common dates in the `Date` format:

```
> d <- data.frame(date = as.Date(cdates, origin = '1970-01-01'))
> str(d)
'data.frame': 998 obs. of  1 variable:
 $ date: Date, format: "2003-01-02" "2003-01-03" ...
```

Next, we need to add the day of the month plus the year and month concatenated to the very same data frame:

```
> d$day <- format(d$date, format = '%d')
> d$my  <- format(d$date, format = '%Y-%m')
```

Now we simply apply the `min` function in each group of `my` (that stands for the same month in the same year) on the `day` variable, which stands for the day of the month:

```
> (fds <- with(d, tapply(day, my, min)))
2003-01 2003-02 2003-03 2003-04 2003-05 2003-06 2003-07 2003-08
   "02"    "03"    "03"    "01"    "01"    "02"    "01"    "01"
2003-09 2003-10 2003-11 2003-12 2004-01 2004-02 2004-03 2004-04
   "02"    "01"    "03"    "01"    "02"    "02"    "01"    "01"
2004-05 2004-06 2004-07 2004-08 2004-09 2004-10 2004-11 2004-12
   "03"    "01"    "01"    "02"    "01"    "01"    "01"    "01"
2005-01 2005-02 2005-03 2005-04 2005-05 2005-06 2005-07 2005-08
   "03"    "01"    "01"    "01"    "02"    "01"    "01"    "01"
2005-09 2005-10 2005-11 2005-12 2006-01 2006-02 2006-03 2006-04
```

```
   "01"      "03"      "01"      "01"      "03"      "01"      "01"      "03"
2006-05 2006-06 2006-07 2006-08 2006-09 2006-10 2006-11 2006-12
   "01"      "01"      "03"      "01"      "01"      "02"      "01"      "01"
```

We have to merge the results with the dates again:

```
> (fds <- as.Date(paste(row.names(fds), fds, sep = '-')))
 [1] "2003-01-02" "2003-02-03" "2003-03-03" "2003-04-01" "2003-05-01"
 [6] "2003-06-02" "2003-07-01" "2003-08-01" "2003-09-02" "2003-10-01"
[11] "2003-11-03" "2003-12-01" "2004-01-02" "2004-02-02" "2004-03-01"
[16] "2004-04-01" "2004-05-03" "2004-06-01" "2004-07-01" "2004-08-02"
[21] "2004-09-01" "2004-10-01" "2004-11-01" "2004-12-01" "2005-01-03"
[26] "2005-02-01" "2005-03-01" "2005-04-01" "2005-05-02" "2005-06-01"
[31] "2005-07-01" "2005-08-01" "2005-09-01" "2005-10-03" "2005-11-01"
[36] "2005-12-01" "2006-01-03" "2006-02-01" "2006-03-01" "2006-04-03"
[41] "2006-05-01" "2006-06-01" "2006-07-03" "2006-08-01" "2006-09-01"
[46] "2006-10-02" "2006-11-01" "2006-12-01"
```

And filter the `res` data frame again to the above identified dates:

```
> res <- lapply(res, function(x) x[which(zoo::index(x) %in% fds)])
```

Then, after merging the list with a time series, it is pretty straightforward to convert the list to the usual `data.frame` format with pretty column names:

```
> res <- do.call(merge, res)
> str(res)
'zoo' series from 2003-01-02 to 2006-12-01
  Data: num [1:48, 1:96] 17.8 15.3 12.1 12.5 15 ...
  Index:  Date[1:48], format: "2003-01-02" "2003-02-03" ...
> res <- as.data.frame(res)
> names(res) <- symbols
```

That would result in a data frame of 48 rows and 96 columns. We still need to compute the returns for each downloaded stock on a column basis, but, to this end, `rft` should also be updated based on the first values in each month:

```
> LIBOR <- LIBOR[LIBOR$Date %in% fds, 'Value']
> rft <- log(1 + head(LIBOR, -1)/36000 * as.numeric(diff(fds)))
> res <- apply(res, 2, riskpremium)
```

Let us also filter the S&P 500 values as a monthly data set:

```
> SP500 <- SP500[SP500$Date %in% fds, 'Adjusted Close']
```

# Modeling the SCL

Using the time series of the stocks' returns, we can calculate the beta for each security. Consequently, we will have the vector of the risk premium as the average of the sample data and a vector containing the betas.

The second regression to be estimated is as follows:

$$\overline{R}_i = \gamma_0 + \gamma_1 \beta_i \qquad (10)$$

Computing the beta for each security and also the mean of the returns in one go can be done with a basic loop after computing the `riskpremium` parameter of each stock and coercing that to make it a `data.frame`:

```
> res <- apply(res, 2, riskpremium)
> res <- as.data.frame(res)
> r <- t(sapply(symbols, function(symbol)
+       c(beta = lm(res[, symbol] ~
+                    riskpremium(SP500))$coefficients[[2]],
+          mean = mean(res[, symbol])))
+ ))
> r <- as.data.frame(r)
```

So, iterating through all symbols, let us plot the returned list of computed betas and the averages of the risk premiums as shown in the following figure:

```
> plot(r$beta, r$mean)
> abline(lm(r$mean ~ r$beta), col = 'red')
```

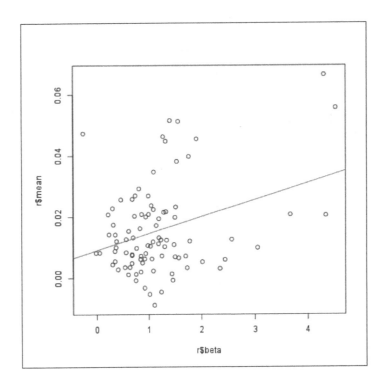

That model can be described as follows:

```
> summary(lm(r$mean ~ r$beta))
```

```
Call:
lm(formula = r$mean ~ r$beta)
```

```
Residuals:
      Min         1Q      Median         3Q        Max
-0.024046  -0.008783  -0.003475   0.006485   0.039731
```

```
Coefficients:
            Estimate Std. Error t value Pr(>|t|)
(Intercept) 0.009084   0.002429   3.740 0.000325 ***
r$beta      0.005528   0.001678   3.295 0.001413 **
---
Signif. codes:  0 '***' 0.001 '**' 0.01 '*' 0.05 '.' 0.1 ' ' 1

Residual standard error: 0.01383 on 89 degrees of freedom
  (5 observations deleted due to missingness)
Multiple R-squared:  0.1087,     Adjusted R-squared:  0.09873
F-statistic: 10.86 on 1 and 89 DF,   p-value: 0.001413
```

According to the above results, the intercept is positive, but it does not differ significantly from zero. The slope of the SML equals to 0.5528% — on a monthly basis — that is slightly lower than expected, as according to the null-hypothesis, it should be the average of the market risk premium of the period: 0.69%. However, this difference is also statistically insignificant. Based on the test, the beta return relationship can not be rejected.

# Testing the explanatory power of the individual variance

The test can be developed further, involving the unsystematic risk tested as a second explanatory variable. The individual risk of a security is to be calculated as follows:

$$\sigma_{ei}^2 = \sigma_i^2 - \beta_i^2 \sigma_m^2 \qquad (11)$$

So, first we have to calculate the vector of the variances, then we get the vector of the individual variances. The regression equation to be estimated is as follows:

$$\overline{R}_i = \gamma_0 + \gamma_1 \beta_i + \gamma_2 \sigma_{ei}^2 \qquad (12)$$

Till now, we update the above loop created for computing the betas and means in `r`:

```
> r <- t(sapply(symbols, function(symbol) {
+     stock <- res[, symbol]
+     beta  <- lm(stock ~ riskpremium(SP500))$coefficients[[2]]
+     c(
+         beta = beta,
```

```
+              mean = mean(stock, na.rm = TRUE),
+              risk = var(stock, na.rm = TRUE) - beta^2 * var(SP500))
+ }))
> r <- as.data.frame(r)
```

Although this loop is almost identical to the previous one, most of the body was rewritten and reformatted based on **DRY (Don't Repeat Yourself)** principles. So, first we have stored the values of symbol in stock and also computed beta before returning the results concatenated with c. Now, we've also added the na.rm = TRUE parameter to the mean and var functions to remove possible missing values before computations. Our model now looks as follows:

```
> summary(lm(r$mean ~ r$beta + r$risk))


Call:
lm(formula = r$mean ~ r$beta + r$risk)


Residuals:
      Min        1Q    Median        3Q       Max
-0.023228 -0.009175 -0.003657  0.006817  0.036262


Coefficients:
              Estimate Std. Error t value Pr(>|t|)
(Intercept)  1.400e-02  3.711e-03   3.772 0.000285 ***
r$beta      -1.743e-03  4.677e-03  -0.373 0.710293
r$risk      -9.956e-08  5.798e-08  -1.717 0.089266 .
---
Signif. codes:  0 '***' 0.001 '**' 0.01 '*' 0.05 '.' 0.1 ' ' 1


Residual standard error: 0.01381 on 93 degrees of freedom
Multiple R-squared:  0.1451,     Adjusted R-squared:  0.1267
F-statistic: 7.891 on 2 and 93 DF,  p-value: 0.0006833
```

Interestingly, the new parameter changed the regression coefficient of beta to negative. On the other hand, however, the risk parameter proved to be insignificant on a 95% significance level. As CAPM concludes that no risk premium is to be paid for diversifiable risk, the null-hypothesis assumes $\beta_2$ to be zero. Here, we cannot reject this hypothesis.

Miller and Scholes (1972) explained the first CAPM tests' results—$\alpha$ differed significantly from zero and the slope was much lower than the average of the market risk premium—with statistical reasons. As the explanatory variable of the second regression (betas) derived from an estimation—from the first regression—it contained statistical error. This estimation bias causes the observed significant intercept and the flatter than expected SML. This statement can be investigated on simulated returns. Further details on simulations can be found in the next two chapters.

# Summary

In this chapter, the systematic risk of asset returns was measured by their contribution to the market's variance—the beta. We used linear regression to quantify this relationship. Hypothesis tests were run in order to confirm the statements of the capital assets pricing model.

# Fixed Income Securities

In *Chapter 3, Asset Pricing Models*, we focused on models establishing a relationship between the risk measured by its beta, the price of financial instruments, and portfolios. The first model, CAPM, used an equilibrium approach, while the second, APT, has built on the no-arbitrage assumption.

The general objective of fixed income portfolio management is to set up a portfolio of fixed income securities with a given risk/reward profile. In other words, portfolio managers are aiming at allocating their funds into different fixed income securities, in a way that maximizes the expected return of the portfolio while adhering to the given investment objectives.

The process encompasses the dynamic modeling of the yield curve, the prepayment behavior, and the default of the securities. The tools used are time series analysis, stochastic processes, and optimization.

The risks of fixed income securities include credit risk, liquidity risk, and market risk among others. The first two can be handled by selecting only securities with predetermined default risk, for example, with a minimum credit rating and with proper liquidity characteristics. The market risk of a fixed income security is generally captured by duration, modified duration, keynote duration, or factor duration. All measures of the interest rate risk a fixed income security faces. This chapter focuses on the market risk of fixed income securities.

# Measuring market risk of fixed income securities

The general formula to obtain the present value of a fixed income security given a yield curve is: $P = \sum_{t=0}^{T} \frac{CF_t}{(1+y_t)^t}$, where $T$ is the time until maturity of the security, $CF_t$ is the cash flow of the security at time $t$, and $y_t$ is the discount rate of a cash flow to be received at time $t$. The market price of the bond will converge to its par value as time passes, even if its yield to maturity remains constant. This price change is expected, hence it is not considered a risk. Market risk arises from the changes in interest rates, which causes reinvestment risk and liquidation risk. The first affects the rate at which coupon payments can be reinvested, and the second impacts the market price of the bond.

The market price impact of interest rate change is measured by examining the price of the bond as a function of its yield to maturity ($y$): $P = \sum_{t=0}^{T} \frac{CF_t}{(1+y)^t}$. Since

$\Delta P = \frac{dP}{dy}\Delta y + \frac{1}{2}\frac{d^2 P}{dy^2}(\Delta y)^2 + ...$, the percentage change of the price caused by a $\Delta y$ change

in yield is expressed as: $\frac{\Delta P}{P} = \frac{1}{P}\frac{dP}{dy}\Delta y + \frac{1}{2}\frac{1}{P}\frac{d^2 P}{dy^2}(\Delta y)^2 + ...$, the second order approximation

of $\Delta P/P$ is $\frac{\Delta P}{P} = -D^*\Delta y + \frac{1}{2}Convexity(\Delta y)^2 = -\frac{D}{1+y}\Delta y + \frac{1}{2}Convexity(\Delta y)^2$. When yields

are expressed periodically, compounded duration ($D$), modified duration ($D^*$), and convexity are defined as follows:

- $D = -\frac{1}{P}\frac{dP}{dy}(1+y) = \sum_{t=0}^{T} t \times \frac{CF_t/(1+y)^t}{P}$

- $D^* = D/(1+y)$

- $Convexity = \frac{1}{P}\frac{d^2 P}{dy^2} = \frac{1}{P}\frac{1}{(1+y)^2}\sum_{t=0}^{T} \frac{CF_t(t^2+t)}{(1+y)^t}$

The pricing formula of the bond shows the obvious inverse relationship between a bond's yield to maturity ($y$) and its price ($P$). Since duration relates to the change in the yield to maturity of the bond to the associated change in its price, it is the most important measure of the bond's interest rate risk. Duration is the weighted average maturity of the bond.

# Example – implementation in R

Consider a 10-year bond with USD 1,000 par value paid at maturity, an annual 8% coupon paid quarterly, and assume that the yield curve is flat at 10% using continuous compounding.

To compute the above described indices, we will use the **GUIDE** package that provides a graphical user interface to various financial calculators and interactive plots for pricing financial derivatives, so in the following examples, most parameters will be set in a more intuitive way compared to the other chapters.

After installing and loading the package, the main program can be started via the GUIDE function:

```
> install.packages('GUIDE')
> library(GUIDE)
> GUIDE()
```

That will load the main window with a menu to access the 55 functions of the package, as shown in the following screenshot:

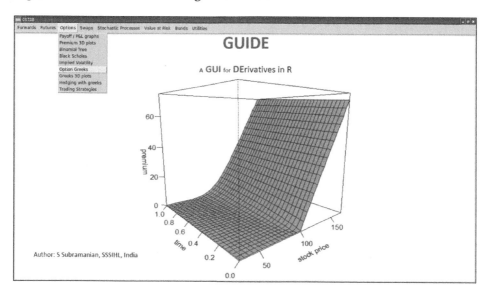

The functions can also be called by direct R commands beside the top menu bar.

The fair value is quickly given by the `bondprice` as USD 867.28. The `priceyield` function demonstrates the inverse relationship between a discount rate and the bond's price. The duration of the bond is determined by `bonddur`, as shown in the following screenshot:

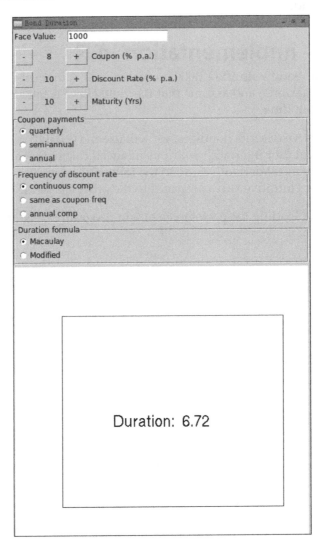

The function can be set to reflect **annual** or **semi-annual Coupon payments**, and the **Frequency of the discount rate** can be varied. The function also allows for the calculation of **Modified Duration**. The **Convexity** of the same bond is calculated by `bondconv`, as shown in the following screenshot:

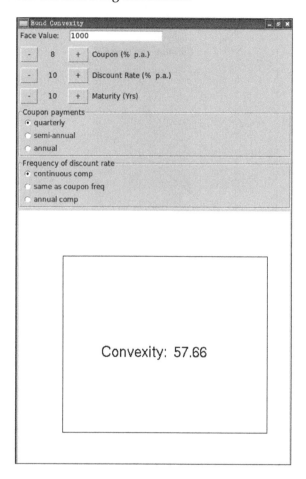

Please note that when discount rates are expressed in continuously compounded yields, the convexity is given by the formula:

$$Convexity = \frac{1}{P}\frac{d^2P}{dy^2} = \frac{1}{P}\sum_{t=0}^{T}CF_t \exp(-yt)t^2$$

The `duryield` and `durcoupon` functions can be used to assess how increasing yield affects duration, and how larger coupon impacts the duration of bonds.

The relationship between **Duration and Maturity** is showed by the `durmaturity` function as displayed in the following screenshot:

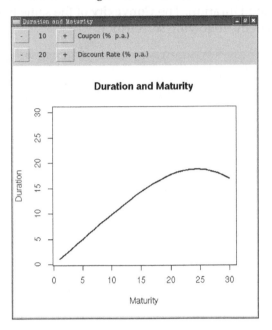

Having calculated the duration or convexity of a bond, a portfolio's duration or convexity is easily computed as the weighted average of the portfolio's individual elements' duration or convexity.

Other packages such as **maRketSim** and **termstrc** also include functions capable of calculating duration, modified duration, and convexity of bonds, or even of entire fixed income portfolios.

# Immunization of fixed income portfolios

A portfolio is immunized when it is unaffected by interest rate change. Duration gives a good measure of interest rate sensitivity; therefore, it is generally used to immunize portfolios. As using duration assumes a flat yield curve and a little parallel shift of the yield curve, the immunized portfolio is constrained by these assumptions, and being unaffected will mean that the value of the portfolio changes only slightly as yields change.

There are two different kinds of immunization strategies: net worth immunization and target date immunization.

# Net worth immunization

Fixed income portfolio managers often have a view on the way the yield curve will change in the future. Let us assume that a portfolio manager expects rates to increase in the near future. As this would have an unfavorable effect on the portfolio, the portfolio manager could decide to set the duration of the portfolio to zero by entering into forward agreements or interest rate swaps. These instruments alter the portfolio's duration and can help in setting the portfolio's duration to zero without having to liquidate the entire portfolio.

Another goal of a portfolio manager can be to set the duration of the portfolio relative to the duration of the portfolio's benchmark. This helps in outperforming the portfolio's benchmark should their anticipation on market movements be justified.

Banks are usually more interested in protecting their equities' value from market price changes. This is carried out by setting their equities' duration to the desired level.

# Target date immunization

Let us consider an investor with a given liability cash flow stream. Immunization of the investor's portfolio will be achieved by constructing an asset portfolio of fixed income securities, with a duration that equals the duration of the liabilities. This target date immunization ensures that future payment obligations will be met from the assets of the portfolio. That process can be addressed by, for example, the `genPortfolio.bond` function.

# Dedication

Dedication is a special kind of target date immunization where the cash flows of the assets are matched with each and every component of the liabilities. One way this can be carried out is by funding the liability components with zero coupon bonds.

# Pricing a convertible bond

Convertible bonds are usually issued by firms with low credit rating and high growth potential. These firms can lower their interest costs by giving the right ( but with no obligation), to the bondholder to convert the bond into a specified number of shares of common stock of the issuing company. The investor receives the potential upside of conversion into equity, while having downside protection with cash flows from the bond. The company benefits from the fact that when the convertibles are converted, the leverage of the company decreases while the trade-off is the stock dilution when the bonds are converted.

These characteristics state that the convertible bonds' behavior has three different stages: in-the-money convertible bonds (conversion price < equity price) behave like equity, at-the-money (conversion price = equity price) convertible bonds are considered as equity and debt, while out-of-the money (conversion price > equity price) convertible bonds show debt-like behavior. Pricing a convertible bond can be complex even within the Black-Scholes-Merton model framework, but the basic principle is pricing the bond and the option separately.

Let us consider a 5-year convertible bond with USD 100 par value, 5% coupon, annual interest payment, and with the right to convert the par at maturity to 4 shares of common stock. Assume that the risk-free rate is 5% for all maturities, the credit spread of the bond is 2%, the price of the underlying stock is USD 20, the volatility of the stock is 20%, and the dividend yield is zero. R can be used to value this convertible bond. First, we define the date for today that will be used in the following example:

```
> today <- Sys.Date()
```

Next, we set the trade and settlement dates and compute the values of the discount curve given a flat yield curve (based on the times argument that is, a sequence between 0 and 10 for now with the step being 0.1):

```
> params <- list(tradeDate  = today - 2,
+                  settleDate = today,
+                  dt         = 0.25)
> times <- seq(0, 10, 0.1)
> dividendYield <- DiscountCurve(params, list(flat = 10e-6), times)
> riskFreeRate  <- DiscountCurve(params, list(flat = 0.05), times)
```

The preceding dividend yield, risk-free rate, and the following fixed underlying asset's price and volatility will be passed to the Black-Scholes process later, which will set up the binomial pricing engine for this bond:

```
> process <- list(
+      underlying = 20,
+      divYield   = dividendYield,
+      rff        = riskFreeRate,
+      volatility = 0.2)
```

We should also specify the conversion ratio, which determines how many shares of the common stock the bondholder would get if he decides to convert his bond to equity. The par value of the bond and the credit spread are also specified here:

```
> bondparams <- list(
+       exercise          = "eu",
+       faceAmount        = 100,
+       redemption        = 100,
+       creditSpread      = 0.02,
+       conversionRatio   = 4,
+       issueDate         = as.Date(today + 2),
+       maturityDate      = as.Date(today + 1825))
```

With annual coupon payments:

```
> dateparams <- list(
+       settlementDays           = 3,
+       dayCounter               = "ActualActual",
+       period                   = "Annual",
+       businessDayConvention    = "Unadjusted")
```

And pass the above specified parameters to the `ConvertibleFixedCouponBond` function:

```
> ConvertibleFixedCouponBond(bondparams, coupon = 0.05, process,
dateparams)
Concise summary of valuation for ConvertibleFixedCouponBond
 Net present value :   107.1013
        clean price :   107.06
        dirty price :   107.1
    accrued coupon :   0.041096
             yield :   0.033848
        cash flows :
      Date     Amount
 2014-06-21    4.9589
 2015-06-21    5.0000
 2016-06-21    5.0073
 2017-06-21    4.9927
 2018-06-21    5.0000
 2018-06-21  100.0000
```

The value of the bond excluding the convertible feature would be approximately USD 92, while the value with the extra feature becomes USD 107.1. Now let us check the change of the net present value if we start to raise the price of the underlying stock from 1 to 30:

```
> res <- sapply(seq(1, 30, 1), function(s) {

+       process$underlying = s

+       ConvertibleFixedCouponBond(bondparams, coupon = 0.05, process,
dateparams)$NPV

+ })
> plot(1:30, res, type = 'l',

+     xlab = 'Price of the underlying stocks',

+     ylab = 'Net Present Value')
```

The following figure shows the relationship between the price of the underlying stock and the calculated value of the convertible bond:

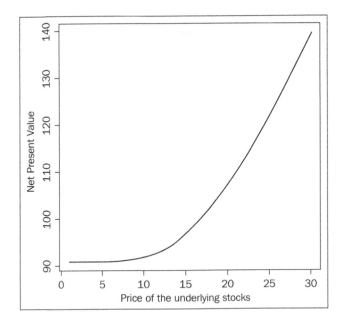

# Summary

In this chapter, we have used R to measure a fixed income portfolio's interest rate risk. We have covered selected functions of the GUIDE package, and applied the convertible bond pricing function of the RQuantLib package. In the next chapter, you'll learn how you can use R for estimating the spot yield curve.

# 5

# Estimating the Term Structure of Interest Rates

In the previous chapter we discussed how changes in the level of interest rates, the term structure, affect the prices of fixed income securities. Now we focus on the estimation of the term structure of interest rates, which is a fundamental concept in finance. It is an important input in almost all financial decisions. This chapter will introduce term structure estimation methods by cubic spline regression, and it will demonstrate how one can estimate the term structure of interest rates using the `termstrc` package and the `govbonds` dataset.

## The term structure of interest rates and related functions

A $t$-year zero-coupon bond with a face value of 1 USD is a security that pays 1 USD at maturity, that is, in $t$ years time. Let $d(t)$ denote its market value, which is also called the $t$-year discount factor. The function $d:[0,T] \to R$ is called the discount function. Based on the no-arbitrage assumption, it is usually assumed that $d(0)=1$, $d(t)$ is monotonically decreasing, and that $d(t)>0$. It is also usually assumed that $d(t)$ is twice continuously differentiable.

Let $r(t)$ denote the continuously compounded annual return of the $t$-year zero coupon bond; it shall be defined as:

$$r(t) = \frac{1}{t} \ln\left(\frac{1}{d(t)}\right)$$

The function $r:[0,T]\rightarrow R$ is called the (zero coupon) yield curve.

Let $f:[0,T]\rightarrow R$ denote the instantaneous forward rate curve or simply the forward rate curve, where:

$$f(t)=\lim_{h\downarrow 0}\frac{\ln|d(t)/d(t+h)|}{h}=-\frac{d'(t)}{d(t)}$$

Here $f(t)$ is the interest rate agreed upon by two parties in a hypothetical forward loan agreement, in which one of the parties commits to lend an amount to the other party in $t$ years time for a very short term and at an interest rate that is fixed when the contract is signed.

The discount function, the yield curve, and the forward rate curve mutually determine each other and are a possible representation of the term structure of interest rates. The term structure may relate to any and all of these functions.

# The estimation problem

We cannot observe the term structure directly, but we can observe the market prices of instruments whose price depends on the term structure and thus estimate the term structure. A good source of information regarding the term structure is the government bond market, where usually a lot of liquid securities are traded whose prices depend solely on the term structure.

Suppose there are $n$ bonds traded whose gross (or dirty) prices are denoted by $p \in R^n$. There are $m$ dates when at least one bond's owners receive a payment. These payments are due in $t_1, t_2, ..., t_m$ years time respectively where $0 < t_1 < ... < t_m = T$. The $n \times m$ matrix C contains the cash flows of the bonds. We model bond prices as the sum of the present value of the bond's cash flow and a normally distributed error term:

$$p = Cd + \varepsilon \qquad (1)$$

Here $d$ is the vector containing the discount factors $d(t_j)$ and $\varepsilon$ is a vector containing the error terms. The observed market price of a bond can differ from the present value of the cash flow for two reasons: there might be a measurement error in the observed market price and/or there might be slight market imperfections, such as transaction costs, which allow for a small difference between the theoretical and the market price, without the difference being an arbitrage opportunity. The variance of the error terms might differ from bond to bond:

$$E(\varepsilon) = 0$$
$$E(\varepsilon\varepsilon') = \sigma^2 \Omega$$

Here, $\Omega$ is an $n \times n$ positive semidefinite diagonal matrix. It is logical to assume that the standard deviation of the error term in the price of a bond is proportional to its bid-ask spread, that is, the difference between the bid and asked price of the bond. Thus, $\omega_{ii}$ is often chosen as the squared bid-ask spread of bond $i$.

Equation *(1)* looks like a typical linear regression, however, it usually cannot be estimated directly as the number of observations (bond prices) is usually less than the number of coefficients to be estimated. Because of this, we need to model the term structure to reduce the number of parameters to be estimated, and to ensure that the resulting term structure estimation is reasonable.

# Estimation of the term structure by linear regression

Suppose that the discount function can be expressed as the linear combination of the $f_1, f_2, ..., f_l$ functions that are twice continuously differentiable functions as

$$d(t) = \sum_{k=1}^{l} w_k f_k(t)$$

where

$$d(0) = \sum_{k=1}^{l} w_k f_k(0) = 1$$

We can estimate the weights $w_k$ by generalized least squares. We will discuss the choice of the functions $f_k$ later. The estimated discount function is the function of the estimated weights $\hat{w}_k$.

$$\hat{d}(t) = \sum_{k=1}^{l} \hat{w}_k f_k(t)$$

Let $D$ denote an $m \times l$ matrix whose elements $d_{jk}$ are $f_k(t_j)$, and $w \in R^l$ be the vector that contains the weights $w_k$. Thus $d = Dw$ and

$$p = CDw + \varepsilon \qquad (2)$$

which is a linear regression model under the constraint that $d(0) = 1$, which can be expressed as follows:

$$r'w = 1 \qquad (3)$$

where $r' = \left( f_1(0), f_2(0), ..., f_l(0) \right)$.

The GLS estimation for the weights of equation (2) under the constraint of equation (3) is

$$\hat{w} = w* - \left( X'\Omega^{-1}X \right)^{-1} r \left[ r' \left( X'\Omega^{-1}X \right)^{-1} r \right]^{-1} (r'w* - 1)$$

where

$$X = CD$$
$$w* = \left( X'\Omega^{-1}X \right)^{-1} X'\Omega^{-1}p$$

# Cubic spline regression

We need to choose the functions $f_k$ carefully if we want the estimation to yield a reasonably estimated discount function. The typical discount function is nonlinear. It is a monotonically decreasing function and converges to zero asymptotically at infinity. Thus, fitting a straight line is not a good idea. One can try to fit a higher order polynomial to the discount function. This is not a satisfactory solution either. If we fit low-order polynomials, they are usually not flexible enough and don't fit well, especially at the short-term maturities. If we fit high-order polynomials, they may fit well but tend to produce wild swings at long-term maturities where relatively few bonds mature. These wild swings usually result in unrealistic term structure estimates.

Spline functions are functions that help solve this problem as their flexibility can be increased locally where needed, without raising the polynomial order of the estimated function. Estimating the term structure by fitting cubic splines to the discount function was first proposed by *McCulloch* in 1971.

Cubic splines are real functions whose domain is an interval of the real line. The domain $[b_0, b_k]$ is divided into subintervals by the so-called knot points $b_0, b_1, \ldots, b_K$ where $b_0 < b_1 < \ldots < b_k$. The cubic spline function is a cubic polynomial on every subinterval, and these cubic polynomials are joined at the knot points so that the spline function is continuous and twice continuously differentiable on $[t, T]$. Every cubic spline function on $[t, T]$ and a given set of knot points $b_0, b_1, \ldots, b_K$ can be expressed as the linear combination of $K + 3$ basis spline functions that are cubic splines over the same knot points. Thus, if we want to fit a cubic spline to the discount function, we simply choose the functions $f_k$ as a cubic spline basis, which we will demonstrate in the German government bonds data from the govbonds dataset.

```
> data(govbonds)
> str(govbonds[['GERMANY']])
List of 8
 $ ISIN        : chr [1:52] "DE0001141414" "DE0001137131" "DE0001141422"
"DE0001137149" ...
 $ MATURITYDATE: Date[1:52], format: "2008-02-15" "2008-03-14" ...
 $ ISSUEDATE   : Date[1:52], format: "2002-08-14" "2006-03-08" ...
 $ COUPONRATE  : num [1:52] 0.0425 0.03 0.03 0.0325 0.0413 ...
 $ PRICE       : num [1:52] 100 99.9 99.8 99.8 100.1 ...
 $ ACCRUED     : num [1:52] 4.09 2.66 2.43 2.07 2.39 ...
 $ CASHFLOWS   :List of 3
  ..$ ISIN: chr [1:384] "DE0001141414" "DE0001137131" "DE0001141422"
"DE0001137149" ...
  ..$ CF  : num [1:384] 104 103 103 103 104 ...
  ..$ DATE: Date[1:384], format: "2008-02-15" "2008-03-14" ...
 $ TODAY       : Date[1:1], format: "2008-01-30"
```

The dataset holds information about 52 German bonds, from which we will concentrate on the issue and maturity dates, price, and provided cash flows. To create a similar dataset ready for further analysis, please see the examples of ?govbonds.

First, we preprocess the bond dataset with the prepro_bond function that returns cash flows, maturities, yield-to-maturity, duration-based weight matrices plus dirty price, and accrued interest vectors, among other values:

```
> prepro <- prepro_bond('GERMANY', govbonds)
```

An important decision is setting the number of knot points and placing them. The first and last knot points are zero and T respectively, and the others are usually chosen so that approximately the same number of bonds mature at every subinterval. Setting the number of knot points is not so straightforward. It will determine the number of parameters to be estimated and will influence the estimated term structure crucially. One could start the estimation process by setting K to 1, then increasing it by one and repeating the estimation until there is significant improvement in goodness of fit and the estimated term structure is well behaved. Alternatively, one can follow the rule of thumb proposed by McCulloch that the number of knot points be $\sqrt{n}$ approximately. We now demonstrate that in the following command with the help of the maturity matrix decomposed from the prepro object:

```
> m <- prepro$m[[1]]
```

And let us define the number of German bonds with n and its rounded square root by s (number of knot points) that results in 7:

```
> n <- ncol(m)
> s <- round(sqrt(n))
```

If s results in a number less than three, identifying the ideal knot points is easy. We will use the following command:

```
> c(floor(min(y[, 1])), max(m[, ncol(m)]))
```

Here we have identified the smallest (min) number in the first column and the largest (max) number from the last (ncol) column from the maturity matrix rounded to the largest integer just below the results (floor).

If s is higher than three, the first and last knot points are defined just as in the preceding command lines and the others between those points are computed with some helper vectors with the length of s-3, as shown in the following commands:

```
> i      <- 2:(s-2)
> h      <- trunc(((i - 1) * n) / (s - 2))
> theta <- ((i - 1) * n) / (s - 2) - h
```

The i vector simply holds the sequence from 2 to 5 in this case, from which we compute the indices of the column (h) from the maturity matrix that will be used to search other knot points. Here theta is used as a weight.

```
> apply(as.matrix(m[, h]), 2, max) +
+     theta * (apply(as.matrix(m[, h + 1]), 2, max) -
+     apply(as.matrix(m[, h]), 2, max))
```

Here we find the highest number in each h$^{th}$ column of the maturity matrix and add the theta-weighted difference of the h+1 and h columns' maximum results in the following output:

```
DE0001135101 DE0001141463 DE0001135218 DE0001135317
    1.006027      2.380274      5.033425      9.234521
```

Now we concatenate (with the c function) the first (minimum) and the last (maximum) value computed earlier to the preceding results copied from the preceding code chunk to identify all knot points:

```
> c(floor(min(y[, 1])), apply(as.matrix(m[, h]), 2, max) + theta *
(apply(as.matrix(m[, h + 1]), 2, max) - apply(as.matrix(m[, h]), 2,
max)), max(m[, ncol(m)]))
```

```
        DE0001135101 DE0001141463 DE0001135218 DE0001135317
0.0000    1.006027      2.380274      5.033425      9.234521  31.44657
```

# Applied R functions

Although we have already used some functions from the termstrc package in the previous example to demonstrate how one can determine the ideal number of knot points and also specify those, this process can be done in an easier manner with some further R functions, as shown in the following command lines:

```
> x <- estim_cs(govbonds, 'GERMANY')
> x$knotpoints[[1]]
        DE0001135101 DE0001141463 DE0001135218 DE0001135317
0.0000    1.006027      2.380274      5.033425      9.234521  31.44657
```

First we used the `estim_cs` function that estimates the term structure of coupon bonds based on cubic splines (*Ferstl-Haydn, 2010*) and returns the knot points in a list with the `knotpoints` name. Please note that `estim_cs` works with a list — just like most functions in the package — that's why `x$knotpoints` returned a list from which we checked only the first element that was identical to the values we computed manually in the preceding section.

There are a bunch of other useful values returned by the preceding function that by default result in the following command lines:

```
----------------------------------------------------
Estimated parameters and robust standard errors:
----------------------------------------------------

[1] "GERMANY:"


t test of coefficients:


          Estimate   Std. Error  t value   Pr(>|t|)
alpha 1   1.9320e-02  1.5230e-02   1.2686    0.2111
alpha 2  -8.4936e-05  3.7926e-03  -0.0224    0.9822
alpha 3  -3.2009e-04  1.1359e-03  -0.2818    0.7794
alpha 4  -3.7101e-04  3.9074e-04  -0.9495    0.3474
alpha 5   7.2921e-04  9.9560e-05   7.3243  3.375e-09 ***
alpha 6   2.0159e-03  1.3019e-04  15.4843  < 2.2e-16 ***
alpha 7  -4.1632e-02  4.5903e-03  -9.0696  1.011e-11 ***
---
Signif. codes:  0 '***' 0.001 '**' 0.01 '*' 0.05 '.' 0.1 ' ' 1
```

The goodness of fit can be shown with the `summary` function, just like with other R models:

```
----------------------------------------------------
Goodness of fit:
----------------------------------------------------


                        GERMANY
RMSE-Prices             0.198573
AABSE-Prices            0.131036
RMSE-Yields (in %)      0.130108
AABSE-Yields (in %)     0.057223
```

The zero-coupon yield curve and its confidence interval can be shown easily with the knot points by simply calling `plot` on the x object.

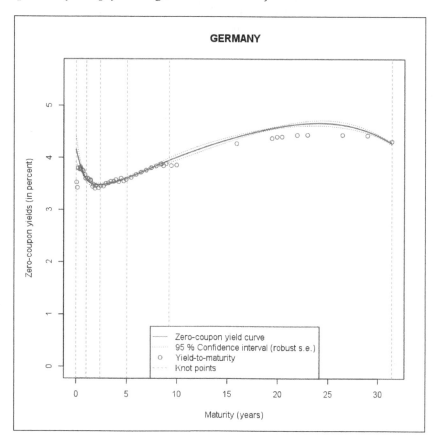

The preceding figure shows the estimated zero-coupon yield curve and the yield-to-maturity of the individual bonds in the database. The two bonds with the shortest maturities are outliers as they are probably less liquid before expiration. We see that the estimated yield curve is very close to the yield to maturity for 10 years. For longer maturities, the estimated zero-coupon yields are typically higher than the corresponding yield to maturity of coupon bonds. It may be the result of an imperfect fit, or it may be explained by the fact that these bonds are not zero-coupon bonds but coupon bonds.

And by setting `mfrow` with `par`, we can also `plot` two different graphs on the same frame (we also set `multiple=TRUE` so that the plots would be rendered without waiting for user input). For example, let us draw the discount and forward curves from the x object using the following commands:

```
> par(mfrow = c(2,1))
> plot(x$discount, multiple = TRUE)
> plot(x$forward, multiple = TRUE)
```

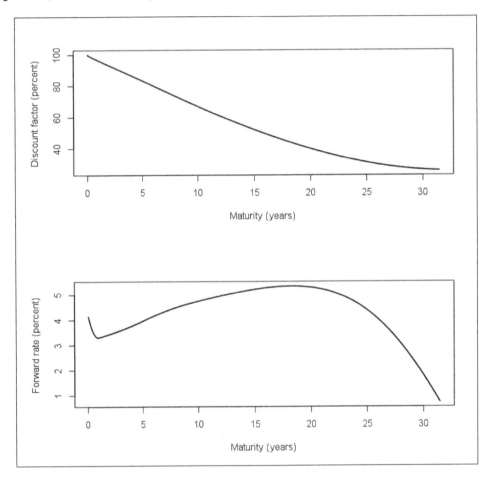

In the preceding figure, we see that the estimated discount function and the forward rate curves are well behaved and do not show the presence of arbitrage opportunities (the discount function is monotonically decreasing, and the forward rate curve does not produce unrealistic values and swings).

The cubic spline estimation of the term structure usually leads to good estimates. Sometimes, however, the estimated term structure is not appealing (the forward rate curve swings widely). In this case, one can use nonlinear spline regression or parsimonious yield curve models, but these are beyond the scope of this chapter.

Further resources such as the Nelson/Siegel, Diebold/Li, Svensson, and Adjusted Svensson methods are also available with the help of the `estim_nss` function or the `YieldCurve` package.

# Summary

In this chapter, we discussed term structure estimation methods by cubic spline regression and also demonstrated how one can estimate the term structure of interest rates in R. After a brief theoretical introduction to term structure and interest rates, also discussing the most basic methods such as a linear regression model and related problems, the chapter gave a detailed overview of an R implementation of cubic spline regression model and also mentioned already published R functions and packages for such tasks with more complex expectations.

# 6
# Derivatives Pricing

Derivatives are financial instruments which derive their value from (or are dependent on) the value of another product, called the **underlying**. The three basic types of derivatives are forward and futures contracts, swaps, and options. In this chapter we will focus on this latter class and show how basic option pricing models and some related problems can be handled in R. We will start with overviewing how to use the continuous Black-Scholes model and the binomial Cox-Ross-Rubinstein model in R, and then we will proceed with discussing the connection between these models. Furthermore, with the help of calculating and plotting of the Greeks, we will show how to analyze the most important types of market risks that options involve. Finally, we will discuss what implied volatility means and will illustrate this phenomenon by plotting the volatility smile with the help of real market data.

The most important characteristics of options compared to futures or swaps is that you cannot be sure whether the transaction (buying or selling the underlying) will take place or not. This feature makes option pricing more complex and requires all models to make assumptions regarding the future price movements of the underlying product. The two models we are covering here differ in these assumptions: the Black-Scholes model works with a continuous process while the Cox-Ross-Rubinstein model works with a discrete stochastic process. However, the remaining assumptions are very similar and we will see that the results are close (moreover, principally identical) too.

# The Black-Scholes model

The assumptions of the Black-Scholes model (*Black and Sholes, 1973*, see also *Merton, 1973*) are as follows:

- The price of the underlying asset ($S$) follows geometric Brownian motion:

  $dS = \mu S dt + \sigma S dW$

  Here $\mu$ (drift) and $\sigma$ (volatility) are constant parameters and $W$ is a standard Wiener process.

- The market is arbitrage-free.
- The underlying is a stock paying no dividends.
- Buying and (short) selling the underlying asset is possible in any (even fractional) amount.
- There are no transaction costs.
- The short-term interest rate (*r*) is known and constant over time.

The main result of the model is that under these assumptions, the price of a European call option (*c*) has a closed form:

- $$c = SN(d1) - Xe^{-r(T-t)}N(d2)$$

- $$d1 = \frac{ln\left(\frac{S}{X}\right) + \left(r + \frac{\sigma^2}{2}\right)(T-t)}{\sigma\sqrt{T-t}},$$

- $$d2 = d1 - \sigma\sqrt{T-t},$$

Here *X* is the strike price, *T-t* is the time to maturity of the option, and *N* denotes the cumulative distribution function of the standard normal distribution. The equation giving the price of the option is usually referred to as the Black-Scholes formula. It is easy to see from put-call parity that the price of a European put option (*p*) with the same parameters is given by:

$$p = Xe^{-r(T-t)}N(-d2) - SN(-d1)$$

Now consider a call and put option on a Google stock in June 2013 with a maturity of September 2013 (that is, with 3 months of time to maturity). Let us assume that the current price of the underlying stock is USD 900, the strike price is USD 950, the volatility of Google is 22%, and the risk-free rate is 2%. We will calculate the value of the call option with the GBSOption function from the **fOptions** package. Beyond the parameters already discussed, we also have to set the cost of carry (b); in the original Black-Scholes model, (with underlying paying no dividends) it equals the risk-free rate.

```
> library(fOptions)
> GBSOption(TypeFlag = "c", S = 900, X =950, Time = 1/4, r = 0.02,
+    sigma = 0.22, b = 0.02)
Title:
 Black Scholes Option Valuation
```

```
Call:
  GBSOption(TypeFlag = "c", S = 900, X = 950, Time = 1/4, r = 0.02,
      b = 0.02, sigma = 0.22)

Parameters:
          Value:
  TypeFlag c
  S         900
  X         950
  Time      0.25
  r         0.02
  b         0.02
  sigma     0.22

Option Price:
  21.79275

Description:
  Tue Jun 25 12:54:41 2013
```

This prolonged output returns the passed parameters with the result just below the `Option Price` label. Setting the `TypeFlag` to p would compute the price of the put option and now we are only interested in the results (found in the `price` slot—see the `str` of the object for more details) without the textual output:

```
> GBSOption(TypeFlag = "p", S = 900, X =950, Time = 1/4, r = 0.02, sigma
= 0.22, b = 0.02)@price
[1] 67.05461
```

Like in the previous chapter, we also have the choice to compute the preceding values with a more user-friendly calculator provided by the **GUIDE** package. Running the `blackscholes()` function would trigger a modal window with a form where we can enter the same parameters. Please note that the function uses the dividend yield instead of cost of carry, which is zero in this case.

# The Cox-Ross-Rubinstein model

The **Cox-Ross-Rubinstein** (CRR) model (*Cox, Ross and Rubinstein, 1979*) assumes that the price of the underlying asset follows a discrete binomial process. The price might go up or down in each period and hence changes according to a binomial tree illustrated in the following plot, where $u$ and $d$ are fixed multipliers measuring the price changes when it goes up and down. The important feature of the CRR model is that $u=1/d$ and the tree is recombining; that is, the price after two periods will be the same if it first goes up and then goes down or vice versa, as shown in the following figure:

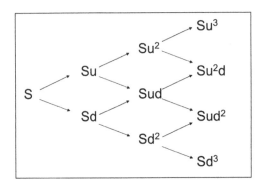

To build a binomial tree, first we have to decide how many steps we are modeling ($n$); that is, how many steps the time to maturity of the option will be divided into. Alternatively, we can determine the length of one time step $\Delta t$, (measured in years) on the tree:

$$\Delta t = \frac{T-t}{n}$$

If we know the volatility ($\sigma$) of the underlying, the parameters $u$ and $d$ are determined according to the following formulas:

$$u = e^{\sigma \sqrt{\Delta t}}$$

And consequently:

$$d = e^{-\sigma \sqrt{\Delta t}}$$

When pricing an option in a binomial model, we need to determine the tree of the underlying until the maturity of the option. Then, having all the possible prices at maturity, we can calculate the corresponding possible option values, simply given by the following formulas:

- $c_T = \max(0, S_T - X)$

- $p_T = \max(0, X - S_T)$

To determine the option price with the binomial model, in each node we have to calculate the expected value of the next two possible option values and then discount it. The problem is that it is not trivial what expected return to use for discounting. The trick is that we are calculating the expected value with a hypothetic probability, which enables us to discount with the risk-free rate. This probability is called risk-neutral probability ($p_n$) and can be determined as follows:

$$p_n = \frac{e^{r\Delta t} - d}{u - d}$$

The interpretation of the risk-neutral probability is quite plausible: if the one-period probability that the underlying price goes up was $p_n$, then the expected return of the underlying would be the risk-free rate. Consequently, an expected value calculated with $p_n$ can be discounted by $r$ and the price of the option in any node of the tree is determined as:

$$g = \left[ p_n g_u + (1 - p_n) g_d \right] e^{-r\Delta t}$$

In the preceding formula, $g$ is the price of an option in general (it may be call or put as well) in a given node, $g_u$ and $g_d$ are the values of this derivative in the two possible nodes one period later.

For demonstrating the CRR model in R, we will use the same parameters as in the case of the Black-Scholes formula. Hence, $S=900$, $X=950$, $\sigma=22\%$, $r=2\%$, $b=2\%$, $T-t=0.25$. We also have to set $n$, the number of time steps on the binomial tree. For illustrative purposes, we will work with a 3-period model:

```
> CRRBinomialTreeOption(TypeFlag = "ce", S = 900, X = 950,
+    Time = 1/4, r = 0.02, b = 0.02, sigma = 0.22, n = 3)@price
[1]  20.33618
> CRRBinomialTreeOption(TypeFlag = "pe", S = 900, X = 950,
+    Time = 1/4, r = 0.02, b = 0.02, sigma = 0.22, n = 3)@price
[1]  65.59803
```

It is worth observing that the option prices obtained from the binomial model are close to (but not exactly the same as) the Black-Scholes prices calculated earlier. Apart from the final result, that is, the current price of the option, we might be interested in the whole option tree as well:

```
> CRRTree <- BinomialTreeOption(TypeFlag = "ce", S = 900, X = 950,
+    Time = 1/4, r = 0.02, b = 0.02, sigma = 0.22, n = 3)
> BinomialTreePlot(CRRTree, dy = 1, xlab = "Time steps",
+    ylab = "Number of up steps", xlim = c(0,4))
> title(main = "Call Option Tree")
```

Here we first computed a matrix by `BinomialTreeOption` with the given parameters and saved the result in `CRRTree` that was passed to the plot function with specified labels for both the x and y axis with the limits of the x axis set from 0 to 4, as shown in the following figure. The y-axis (number of up steps) shows how many times the underlying price has gone up in total. Down steps are defined as negative up steps.

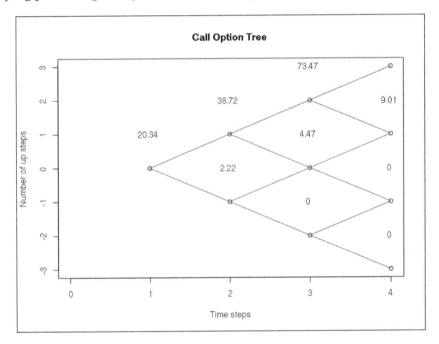

The European put option can be shown similarly by changing the `TypeFlag` to `pe` in the previous code:

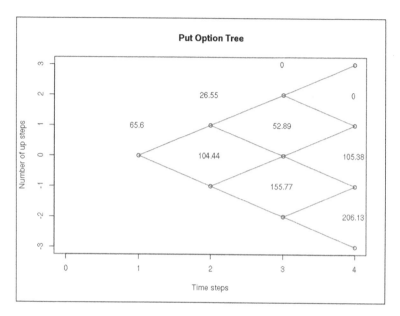

# Connection between the two models

After applying the two basic option pricing models, we give some theoretical background to them. We do not aim to give a detailed mathematical derivation, but we intend to emphasize (and then illustrate in R) the similarities of the two approaches. The financial idea behind the continuous and the binomial option pricing is the same: if we manage to hedge the option perfectly by holding the appropriate quantity of the underlying asset, it means we created a risk-free portfolio. Since the market is supposed to be arbitrage-free, the yield of a risk-free portfolio must equal the risk-free rate. One important observation is that the correct hedging ratio is holding $\partial g / \partial S$ underlying asset per option. Hence, the ratio is the partial derivative (or its discrete correspondent in the binomial model) of the option value with respect to the underlying price. This partial derivative is called the delta of the option. Another interesting connection between the two models is that the delta-hedging strategy and the related arbitrage-free argument yields the same pricing principle: the value of the derivative is the risk-neutral expected value of its future possible values, discounted by the risk-free rate. This principle is easily tractable on the binomial tree where we calculated the discounted expected values node by node; however, the continuous model has the same logic as well, even if the expected value is mathematically more complicated to compute. This is the reason why we gave only the final result of this argument, which was the Black-Scholes formula.

Now we know that the two models have the same pricing principles and ideas (delta-hedging and risk-neutral valuation), but we also observed that their numerical results are not equal. The reason is that the stochastic processes assumed to describe the price movements of the underlying asset are not identical. Nevertheless, they are very similar; if we determine the value of $u$ and $d$ from the volatility parameter as we did it in *The Cox-Ross-Rubinstein model* section, the binomial process approximates the geometric Brownian motion. Consequently, the option price of the binomial model converges to that of the Black-Scholes model if we increase the number of time steps (or equivalently, decrease the length of the steps).

To illustrate this relationship, we will compute the option price in the binomial model with increasing numbers of time steps. In the following figure, we compare the results with the Black-Scholes price of the option:

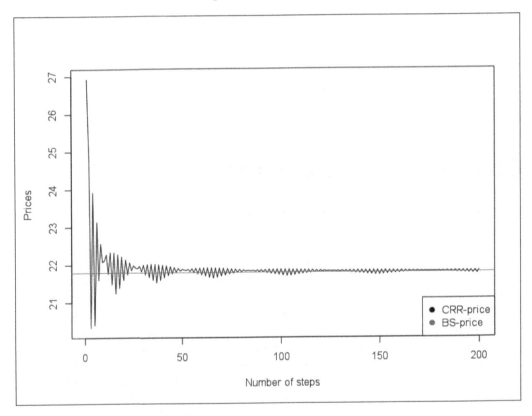

The plot was generated by a loop running N from 1 to 200 to compute CRRBinomialTreeOption with fixed parameters:

```
> prices <- sapply(1:200, function(n) {
+   CRRBinomialTreeOption(TypeFlag = "ce", S = 900, X = 950,
+     Time = 1/4, r = 0.02, b = 0.02, sigma = 0.22, n = n)@price
+ })
```

Now the prices variable holds 200 computed values:

```
> str(prices)
 num [1:200] 26.9 24.9 20.3 23.9 20.4...
```

Let us also compute the option with the generalized Black-Scholes option:

```
> price <- GBSOption(TypeFlag = "c", S = 900, X = 950, Time = 1/4, r =
0.02, sigma = 0.22, b = 0.02)@price
```

And show the prices in a joint plot with the GBS option rendered in red:

```
> plot(1:200, prices, type='l', xlab = 'Number of steps',
+     ylab = 'Prices')
> abline(h = price, col ='red')
> legend("bottomright", legend = c('CRR-price', 'BS-price'),
+     col = c('black', 'red'), pch = 19)
```

# Greeks

Understanding the risk-types that an option might involve is crucial for all market participants. The idea behind Greeks is to measure the different types of risks; they represent the sensitivity of the option to different factors. The Greeks of a plain vanilla option are: delta ($\Delta$, sensitivity to the underlying price), gamma ($\Gamma$, sensitivity of delta to the underlying price, delta of delta), theta ($\theta$, sensitivity to time), rho ($\rho$, sensitivity to the risk-free rate), and vega ($V$, sensitivity to the volatility). In terms of mathematics, all Greeks are partial derivatives of the derivative price:

- $\Delta = \dfrac{\partial g}{\partial S}$

- $\Gamma = \dfrac{\partial^2 g}{\partial S^2}$

- $\theta = \dfrac{\partial g}{\partial t}$

- $\rho = \dfrac{\partial g}{\partial r}$

- $V = \dfrac{\partial g}{\partial \sigma}$

The Greeks can be computed easily for each option with the GBSGreeks function:

```
> sapply(c('delta', 'gamma', 'vega', 'theta', 'rho'), function(greek)
+    GBSGreeks(Selection = greek, TypeFlag = "c", S = 900, X = 950,
+       Time = 1/4, r = 0.02, b = 0.02, sigma = 0.22)
+ )
     delta         gamma          vega         theta           rho
0.347874404   0.003733069 166.308230868 -79.001505841   72.82355323
```

It is often useful to analyze how a given Greek changes if some market parameters change. Such analysis might help us to understand risks better. For example, delta of a call option as a function of the underlying price is an increasing curve taking an S shape, ranging from 0 to 1. These characteristics are always valid, but if time passes and we are approaching the maturity of the option, the curve becomes steeper and steeper (see the next figure). The interpretation is as follows: if it is very probable that the call option will be exercised, then it is very similar to a long forward contract; hence, delta is close to 1. If the chance of exercising is very low, holding the call option is similar to holding nothing and delta is 0. As time passes, the interval of those underlying prices where the exercising is really uncertain (that is, neither very probable, nor very improbable) gets narrower; as a result, the curve of the delta becomes steeper. To illustrate this behavior, we will plot the delta of a call as a function of the underlying price, with three different maturities.

To compute the deltas, we run two loops: one with three different time values and s running from 500 to 1500:

```
> deltas <- sapply(c(1/4, 1/20, 1/50), function(t)
+              sapply(500:1500, function(S)
+                GBSGreeks(Selection = 'delta', TypeFlag = "c",
+          S = S, X = 950, Time = t, r = 0.02, b = 0.02, sigma = 0.22)))
```

The resulting deltas holds 1001 rows (for the s values) and three columns (for the specified times) that we show in a joint plot:

```
> plot(500:1500, deltas[, 1], ylab = 'Delta of call option',
+    xlab = "Price of the underlying (S)", type = 'l')
> lines(500:1500, deltas[, 2], col='blue')
> lines(500:1500, deltas[, 3], col='red')
> legend("bottomright", legend = c('t=1/4', 't=1/20', 't=1/50'),
+    col = c('black', 'blue', 'red'), pch = 19)
```

The following figure shows the delta of the call options with three different values of time to maturity:

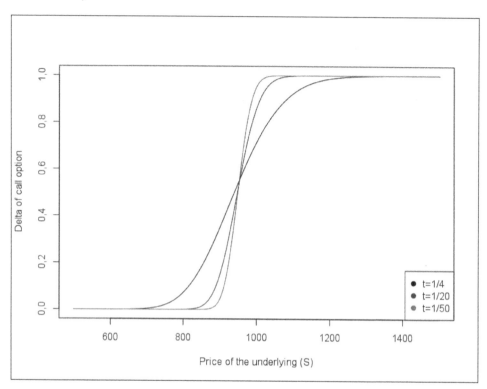

Determining or plotting the Greeks of complex option strategies is very similar. For example, calculating the delta of a straddle position (a portfolio of a call and a put option with the same parameters) means simply calculating deltas separately for the call and the put and then adding them. We will plot delta of a straddle as a function of the underlying price. We may observe that the shape is very similar to the delta of the previous call, but now the S-curve is ranging from -1 to 1:

```
> straddles <- sapply(c('c', 'p'), function(type)
+                 sapply(500:1500, function(S)
+                     GBSGreeks(Selection = 'delta', TypeFlag = type, S = S,
X = 950, Time = 1/4, r = 0.02, b = 0.02, sigma = 0.22)))
```

So we call a nested loop running s from 500 to 1500 for both the call and put options keeping the other parameters fixed, and save the resulting deltas in a matrix. With the next command, the sum of these rows (put and call options) is rendered:

```
> plot(500:1500, rowSums(straddles), type='l',
+   xlab='Price of the underlying (S)', ylab = 'Delta of straddle')
```

The resulting plot illustrates the delta of a straddle position as a function of the underlying's price as shown in the following figure:

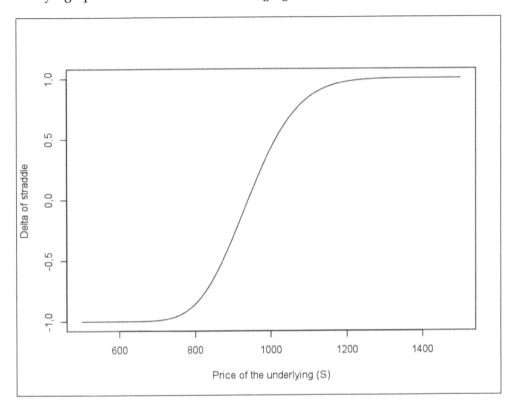

# Implied volatility

The Black-Scholes model is often criticized because of some shortcomings. One important problem is that the model assumes constant volatility for the underlying asset, which does not hold in reality. Furthermore, since it is not observable directly, the `volatility` is the most complicated parameter of the model to calibrate. Due to this difficulty, the Black-Scholes formula is often used in an indirect way for estimating the `volatility` parameter; we observe the market price of an option, then in view of all the other parameters we can search for $\sigma$ that results a Black-Scholes price equal to the observed market price. This $\sigma$ parameter is called the implied volatility of the option. As Riccardo Rebonato famously stated, implied volatility is "the wrong number to put in the wrong formula to get the right price" (*Rebonato, 1999, p.78*).

We will illustrate the calculation of implied volatility with the help of some Google options. The options are call options with the maturity of September 21, 2013 and strike prices ranging from USD 700 to USD 1150 (76 different options). We collected the ask prices of these options on June 25, 2013 from finance.google.com and put them in a CSV file. For the calculations, we need to know that the price of Google on the given day was USD 866.2. Since the time to maturity is 88 days, we will use 88/360 years for the Time parameter. The risk-free rate and the cost of carry are assumed to remain 2% further on.

First, load the Google options from a CSV file:

```
> goog <- read.csv('goog_calls.csv')
```

And then run a loop for each line of the dataset to compute the volatility with the given parameters:

```
> volatilites <- sapply(seq_along(goog$Strike), function(i)
+   GBSVolatility(price = goog$Ask.Price[i], TypeFlag = "c",
+   S = 866.2, X = goog$Strike[i], Time = 88/360, r = 0.02, b = 0.02))
```

The volatilities variable is a vector holding the computed values:

```
> str(volatilites)
 num [1:76] 0.258 0.253 0.269 0.267 0.257...
```

That can be shown against the strike price:

```
> plot(x = goog$Strike, volatilites, type = 'p',
+     ylab = 'Implied volatiltiy', xlab = 'Strike price (X)')
```

Hence, the following figure shows the implied volatilities for different strike prices:

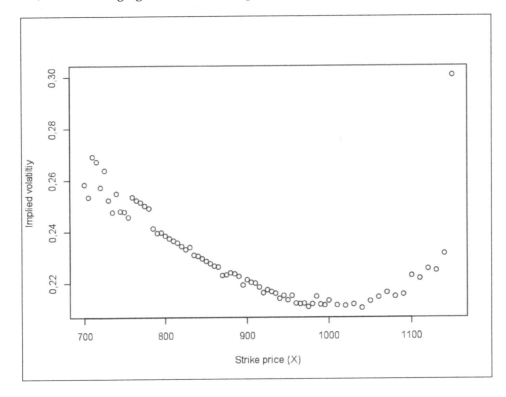

It is worth noticing that the implied volatilities calculated for Google options vary according to the strike prices. This is contrary with the Black-Scholes model, which assumes constant volatility. The observed implied volatility pattern (lower volatilities for medium strike prices) is not unique and appears in financial markets quite frequently. Because of the specific form of the curve, the phenomenon is called the volatility smile.

# Summary

In this chapter, we have used R to price plain vanilla options with the Black-Scholes and Cox-Ross-Rubinstein models. Furthermore, we examined the basic Greeks and the implied volatility of these options. For more details on the financial background of these topics, see (*Hull, 2011*). Besides getting to know some tools from the fOptions package, we have also created a few loops and custom functions programmatically for simulation purposes. The next chapter will concentrate on how to manage credit risks by various models such as choosing an optimal credit portfolio with Monte-Carlo simulation and credit scoring methods.

# 7
# Credit Risk Management

This chapter introduces some useful tools for credit risk management. Credit risk is the distribution of the financial losses due to unexpected changes in the credit quality of a counterparty in a financial agreement (*Giesecke 2004*). Several tools and industrial solutions were developed for managing credit risk. In accordance with the literature, one may consider credit risk as the **default risk, downgrade risk,** or **counterparty risk**. In most cases, the default risk is related directly to the risk of non-performance of a claim or credit. In contrast, downgrade risk arises when the price of a bond declines due to its worsening credit rating without any realized credit event. Counterparty risk means the risk when the counterparty of a contract does not meet the contractual obligations. However, the contractual or regulatory definition of a credit event can usually be wider than just a missed payment. The modeling end estimation of the possibility of default is an essential need in all of the three cases.

Managing credit risk is conducted in various ways at financial institutions. In general, the tasks in credit risk management are as follows:

- Credit portfolio selection (for example, the decision of a commercial bank about lending or credit scoring)

- Measuring and predicting the probability of default or downgrade (using, for example, a credit rating migration matrix with CreditMetrics)

- Modeling the distribution of the financial loss due to default or downgrade (for a single entity: structural and reduced form pricing and risk models or, for a portfolio: dependency structure modeling)

- Mitigating or eliminating credit risk (with a hedge, diversification, prevention, or insurance; we do not investigate it in this book)

In this chapter, we will show examples using R for some of the preceding listed problems. At first, we introduce the basic concepts of credit loss modeling, namely, the structural and reduced form approaches, and their applications in R. After that, we provide a practical way correlated random variables with copulas, which is a useful technique of structured credit derivative pricing. We also illustrate how R manages credit migration matrices and, finally, we give detailed insight into credit scoring with analysis tools, such as logit and probit regressions and **receiver operating characteristic (ROC)** analysis.

# Credit default models

The goal of the first part of the chapter is to show the methods of using R for pricing and performing Monte Carlo simulations with standard credit risk models. The following sections give an essential picture of loss distributions and the generating and pricing of a single debt instrument.

# Structural models

We start with the well-known option-based model of Merton (*Merton 1974*) as the introductory model of structural approach. Merton evaluates risky debt as a contingent claim of the firm value. Let us suppose that the V firm value follows geometric Brownian motion:

$$dV_t = \mu V_t + \sigma V_t dW_t$$

In the preceding formula, $\mu$ is the drift parameter, $\sigma > 0$ is the volatility parameter, dW is the differential of the Wiener process, and the initial asset value is $V_0 > 0$. The model assumes a flat yield curve, with r as the constant interest rate, and lets us define the default state as that where the value of the assets V falls below the liabilities (K) upon the of maturity of debt (T). We express the $V_T$ firm value at maturity as the integral of:

$$V_T = V_0 \exp\left(\int_0^T dlnV_t\right)$$

Where we express $dlnV_t$ using Ito's lemma to derive the differential of the logarithm of firm value as:

$$dlnV_t = \left(\mu - \frac{\sigma^2}{2}\right)dt + \sigma dW_t$$

Along with generating Gaussian distributed random variables for capturing $\Delta W \sim \sqrt{\Delta t}\, N(0,1)$, we calculate the $V_T$ firm value at maturity with this discrete approach in the following way:

$$V_T = V_0 exp\left( \sum_{i=1}^{M}\left( \mu - \frac{\sigma^2}{2}\right)\Delta t + \sigma \Delta W_i \right)$$

Where $\Delta t$ denotes the one-period length of the elapsed time. We simulate the firm value with R in accordance with this logic. First, set the parameters of the simulation, namely, the initial asset value, the drift, and the volatility parameters in the following way:

```
> V0 <- 100; nu <- 0.1; sigma <- 0.2
```

Next, declare the length of $\Delta t$ and the end of the time periods (Time):

```
> dt <- 1 / 252; Time <- 1
```

Let's also compute the number of time periods:

```
> M <- Time / dt
```

And finally, decide on the number of generated trajectories:

```
> n <- 10000
```

To make pseudo-random generated variables you would be able to replicate later, set a random seed every time before calling the generator functions:

```
> set.seed(117)
```

And, to produce the increments of the logarithm of the V process ($\Delta$lnV), generate n*M numbers from a normal distribution using the specified mean and standard deviation:

```
> val  <- rnorm(n*M,
+    mean = (nu - sigma^2 / 2) * dt,
+    sd   = sigma * dt^0.5)
```

And store these numbers in a matrix with M rows and n columns:

```
> dlnV <- matrix(val, M, n)
```

In order to get the variation of the firm value in time (v), summarize the logarithm of the increments and, as computed above, take the exponential of this sum and multiply it with the initial firm value. The equivalent code for n number of trajectories is as follows:

```
> V <- V0 * exp(apply(dlnV, 2, cumsum))
```

The used `cumsum` function is common with the `apply` command. Plot the first five trajectories with `matplot` as follows:

```
> matplot(x = seq(0 + dt, Time, dt), y = V[, 1:5], type = 's', lty = 1,
+    xlab = 'Time',
+    ylab = 'Firm value trajectories',
+    main = 'Trajectories of firm values in the Merton model')
```

We selected the first five (`1:5`) columns of v to be plotted with solid (`lty=1`) and stair steps (`type='s'`) lines resulting in the following graph:

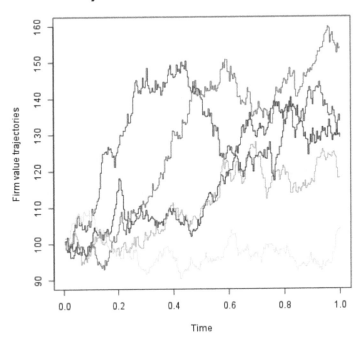

Note that the price of the risky debt is the expected value of the discounted payoff of the risky debt at maturity as per the risk neutral or martingale P measure, where drift is the `r` risk-free interest rate as the following formula expresses:

$$D = E^P \left[ e^{-rT} \min(V_T, K) \right]$$

If we set the `r` risk-free interest rate and face value of the debt (`K`):

```
> r <- 0.05; K <- 80
```

We can demonstrate the Monte Carlo pricing as the parallel min (`pmin`) of the debt face value and the previously computed `v` from which we take the $M^{th}$ column's mean as shown in the previous formula, as follows:

```
> D <- exp(-r * Time) * mean((pmin(V[M, ], K)))
```

For the standard parameters and the fixed pseudo-random generated variables `D`, risky debt with a face value of 80 dollars counts:

```
> D
[1] 75.73553
```

From the Black-Scholes pricing formula of the European call options, the value of risky debt value at `t=0` can be expressed as the `v` firm value less the equity value (`E`), which is a European call option on `v`. Noting the pricing formula with $c^{BS}$, we get:

$$D = V - c^{BS}(V, K, r, \sigma, T)$$

One can calculate debt value with the `GBSOption` function of the `fOptions` package. After installing and calling the following library, one can use the following appropriate function:

```
> install.packages("fOptions"); library(fOptions)
```

Set the `TypeFlag` parameter to `"c"` (call) and the other parameters to the previously defined value. Select parameter `b` to the `r` risk-free interest rate to get the Black-Scholes European call and write the `@price` slot at the end of the command to return the value of `price` from the generated object of class `fOption`:

```
> V0 - GBSOption(TypeFlag = "c", S = V0, X = K, Time = Time, r = r,
+
b =
r, sigma = sigma)@price
```

We receive the following result, which is very close to our previous estimation:

```
[1] 75.41116
```

However, there is a small difference between analytically and numerically computed prices; with the increasing number of trajectories and decreasing `Δt`, the price based upon Monte Carlo simulation converges to the theoretical price. Let us calculate the term structure of credit spreads (denoted by `s(T)`) on risky debt at `t=0` as follows, where credit spreads depend on the maturity of debt (`T`):

$$s(T) = \frac{1}{T} \ln\left(\frac{K}{D}\right) - r$$

For different maturities (from 0.1 to 10 years by 0.1 year), plot these spreads in a hump-shaped curve. Define the time grids as follows:

```
> Time <- seq(0.1, 10, 0.1)
```

And recalculate the debt value for each point on the grid to calculate the credit spreads:

```
> D <- V0 - GBSOption(TypeFlag = "c", S = V0, X = K, Time = Time, r = r,
+
b = r,

sigma = sigma)@price
```

It is useful to plot this curve:

```
> matplot(x = Time, y = creditspreads, type = 'l', xlab = 'Maturity',
+      ylab = 'Credit spreads',
+      main = 'Term structure of credit spreads in the Merton model')
```

The following figure shows the team structure of credit spreads in the Merton Model:

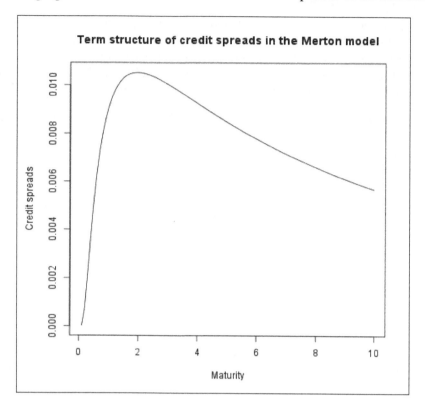

There are several extensions of Merton's model, for example, Moody's KMV application or the Black and Cox first hitting the time approach.

# Intensity models

The second common and popular approach for modeling credit defaults is the intensity-based (reduced form) modeling. In this framework, we assume that the default occurs without showing any earlier sign for predictability. The dynamics of the default intensity depend on the predicted probability of default. We also show an example later in the chapter, where intensity is constant.

The central idea behind the intensity models is that the number of independent defaults in a given time interval comes from the Poisson distribution. Let $\tau_1$, $\tau_2$, ..., $\tau_i$, ..., $\tau_n$ be random default times. Thus, let $N_t$ denote the number of defaults up to time t as follows:

$$N_t = \sum_{i=1}^{\infty} 1_{\tau_i \le t}$$

Where the indicator function formulates the following:

$$1_{\tau_i \le t} = \begin{cases} 1, & if\ \tau_i \le t \\ 0, & otherwise \end{cases}$$

The probability that the number of jumps equals to k on the [s,t] interval is derived from the Poisson distribution where $\lambda_u$ is the instantaneous intensity of default at time u:

$$Prob\left(N_t - N_s = k \mid F_s\right) = \frac{1}{k!}\left(\int_s^t \lambda_u du\right)^k e^{-\int_s^t \lambda_u du}$$

The probability of default occurring before time t is the expected value of the following generalization exponential cumulative distribution function:

$$Prob\left(\tau \le t \mid F_0\right) = E^P\left(1 - e^{-\int_0^t \lambda_s ds} \mid F_0\right)$$

However, though elementary models use a constant $\lambda$ hazard rate, industrial models apply more complex structures. For example, in the double-stochastic Poisson model (or Cox-model), the hazard rate follows the Cox-Ingersoll-Ross process described in the following equation:

$$d\lambda = \left(\theta_1 - \theta_2 \lambda_t\right)dt + \theta_3\sqrt{\lambda_t}\,dW$$

A simulation of the **Cox-Ingersoll-Ross (CIR)** process is supplied by the `sde` package:

```
> library(sde)
```

Redefine the time dimensions, maturity, length, and number of time periods:

```
> Time <- 1; dt <- 1/252; M <- Time / dt
```

After that, create the CIR process by declaring the X0 initial value, the $\theta_1$, $\theta_2$ drift parameters ($\theta_1/\theta_2$ is the long run value, $\theta_2$ is the speed of adjustment), and the $\theta_3$ volatility parameter:

```
> lambda <- sde.sim(X0 = 0.1, delta = dt,T = Time, N = M,
+       theta = c (0.05, 0.5, 0.2), model = "CIR")
```

It is easy to produce Poisson processes in R. Let us generate `n* (M+1)` Poisson distributed random variables (n is the number of trajectories), with a `lambda` parameter vector (this simulated vector of $\theta$ proves that the process is a double-stochastic or Cox process):

```
> n <- 5
> set.seed(117); val <- rpois(n * (M + 1), lambda)
```

Store these numbers in a `matrix` with M+1 rows and n columns, such as the following:

```
> dN <- matrix(val, M + 1, n)
```

Add the increments of $N_t$ (dN) to get the whole Cox process (N):

```
> N <- apply(dN, 2, cumsum)
```

Plot it as we did earlier in the chapter. The resulting graph should look something like the following diagram.

```
> matplot(x = seq(0, Time, dt), y = N[, 1:5], type = 's', xlab = 'Time',
+     ylab = "'Number of defaults' process trajectories",
+     main = 'Trajectories of Cox processes ')
```

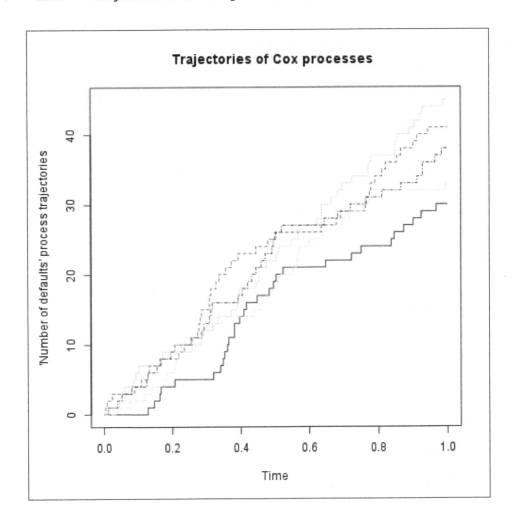

# Correlated defaults – the portfolio approach

In this section, we show you how to deal with correlated random variables with copulas for the simulation of loss distributions of credit portfolios. The **copula** function is a joint cumulative distribution function of uniform distributed random variables. The **copula** function contains all the information on the dependence structure of the components. Any of the continuously distributed random variables can be transformed into uniformly distributed variables, which allows for the possibility of general modeling; for example, it can be combined with the structural approach. Using the `copula` package, we demonstrate how to simulate two uniformly distributed random variables with Gaussian and t-copulas, and how to fit in a Gaussian copula parameter from the generated data. (One can apply this method for historical datasets also.) This package also serves useful functions in a wide range of topics about copulas, such as plotting or fitting copula classes involving Archimedean copulas.

At first, declare a Gaussian copula class with an `0.7` correlation after loading the `copula` package as follows:

```
> library(copula)
> norm.cop <- normalCopula(0.7)
```

After that, generate `500` realizations of two uniformly distributed random variables with the Gaussian copula dependency structure:

```
> set.seed(117); u1 <- rCopula(500, norm.cop)
```

For the comparison, define a `tcopula` class with an `0.7` correlation and `4` degrees of freedom:

```
> t.cop <- tCopula(0.7, df = 4)
```

Now, generate `500` realizations of pairs of random variables with t-copula dependence:

```
> set.seed(117); u2 <- rCopula(500, t.cop)
```

Plot the results into two graphs next to each other. The par command ensures the two figures will be placed next to each other, ordered in a row and two columns (mfcol).

```
> par(mfcol = c(1, 2))
> plot(u1, main = 'Scatter graphs of random variable pairs generated by
Gaussian copula')
> plot(u2, main = 'Scatter graphs of random variable pairs generated by
t-copula')
```

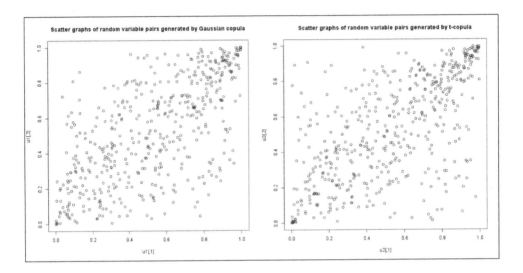

Fit the Gaussian copula correlation parameter for u1 data with the maximum likelihood (ml) method where the function uses the copula family type of the norm.cop object we defined before:

```
> fit.ml <- fitCopula(norm.cop, u1, method = "ml")
```

When we print the following results, we receive that the estimated correlation is around 0.69:

```
> fit.ml
fitCopula() estimation based on 'maximum likelihood'
and a sample of size 500.
      Estimate Std. Error z value Pr(>|z|)
rho.1  0.68583    0.01936   35.43   <2e-16 ***
---
Signif. codes:  0 '***' 0.001 '**' 0.01 '*' 0.05 '.' 0.1 ' ' 1
```

```
The maximized loglikelihood is  164.8

Optimization converged

Number of loglikelihood evaluations:

function gradient

       28        3
```

We remark that the package supports some other methods for estimating correlation.

# Migration matrices

Credit rating transition is the migration of a corporate or governmental bond from one rating to another. The well-known industrial application is the CreditMetrics approach. It provides a risk modeling tool for bond portfolios to estimate the **Conditional Value-at-Risk (CVaR)** and credit spreads of a portfolio due to downgrade and upgrading. In this section, we show how to calculate credit spreads from a transition matrix.

We have to define the **loss given default (lgd)**, the ratings (in this example: A, B, and D) and the one year transition matrix to compute credit spreads:

```
> library(CreditMetrics)
> lgd <- 0.5
> rc <- c( "A", "B", "D")
> M <- matrix(c(85, 13, 2, 5, 80, 15, 0, 0, 100 ) /100, 3, 3,
+             dimnames = list(rc, rc), byrow = TRUE)
```

The command cm.cs calculates the credit spreads from the migration matrix:

```
> cm.cs(M, lgd)
          A          B
0.01005034 0.07796154
```

According to this example, a debt instrument with the rating "A" has around 1% credit spread and debt rated "B" has around 7.8% credit spread, calculated from the M migration matrix.

# Getting started with credit scoring in R

R provides powerful statistical tools for credit scoring. We emphasize here some of the most common techniques, namely probability default estimation with logit and probit regressions and ROC curve analysis. During both behavioral and application credit scoring, one can estimate or score the probability of default in the usual way that the theory of cross-sectional econometrics suggests.

Logit and probit regressions are generalized linear regression models with binary, dependent variables, where the two outcomes can be, for example, either defaulted or not. Logit regression uses logistic function; the probit model applies a cumulative distribution function of the standard normal distribution for estimating the probability of default. Coefficients of independent variables are typically estimated by the maximum likelihood method in both cases. Logit and probit regression models can be called with the `glm` command, which is the generalized linear model function in R for estimating coefficients. Typical R tools for regression analysis suit further examinations well. For example, the `anova` function is also useful in providing a classical analysis of variance.

Credit scoring modelers often employ receiver operating characteristic curves to illustrate the performance of their estimated model. The ROC curve shows the ratio of the sensitivity (sensitivity: accepted non-defaulted, to all non-defaulted) to one minus the specificity (specificity: denied defaulted, to all defaulted). The `pROC` package contains the `roc` function for producing the ROC curve. The well-documented package can be installed in the usual way and the ROC curve can be plotted with the `plot` command.

# Summary

In this chapter, we briefly introduced some of the most common methods related to credit risk modeling. However, there are several industrial approaches for handling default risk. The bases of the advanced methods are usually some of the structural and intensity-based approaches. Copula models are still popular for modeling the risk of credit portfolios, especially in the pricing of structured credit derivatives. There are comprehensive and strong R packages for modeling copulas. The first step to model downgrade risk is knowledge about the principles of managing migration matrices and the CreditMetrics approach. Finally, we briefly outlined the possibilities of credit scoring in R.

# 8

# Extreme Value Theory

The risk of extreme losses is at the heart of many risk management problems both in insurance and finance. An extreme market move might represent a significant downside risk to the security portfolio of an investor. Reserves against future credit losses need to be sized to cover extreme loss scenarios in a loan portfolio. The required level of capital for a bank should be high enough to absorb extreme operational losses. Insurance companies need to be prepared for losses arising from natural or man-made catastrophes, even of a magnitude not experienced before.

**Extreme Value Theory (EVT)** is concerned with the statistical analysis of extreme events. The methodology provides distributions that are consistent with extreme observations and, at the same time, have parametric forms that are supported by theory. EVT's theoretical considerations compensate the unreliability of traditional estimates (caused by sparse data on extremes). EVT allows the quantification of the statistics of extreme events, possibly even beyond the most extreme observation so far.

The types of models within EVT that find the most applications in finance and insurance are the models of **threshold exceedances**. These characterize the distribution of all large observations that exceed some high level, thus providing an estimate of the *tail* of the distribution. Since many risk management problems can be formulated in terms of the tails of distributions, these models may be directly applied to such problems.

The objective of this chapter is to present possible uses of Extreme Value Theory in insurance and finance through the example of a real-life risk management application. First, we provide a brief overview of the theory of threshold exceedance models in EVT. We then work through a detailed example of fitting a model to the tails of the distribution of fire losses. We use the fitted model to calculate high quantiles (Value at Risk) and conditional expectations (Expected Shortfall) for the fire losses.

# Theoretical overview

Let the random variable $X$ represent the random loss that we would like to model, with $F(x) = P(X \leq x)$ as its distribution function. For a given threshold $u$, the excess loss over the threshold $Y = X - u$ has the following distribution function:

$$F_u(y) = P(X - u \leq y \mid X > u) = \frac{F(y+u) - F(u)}{1 - F(u)}$$

For a large class of underlying loss distributions, the $F_u(y)$ distribution of excess losses over a high threshold $u$ converges to a **Generalized Pareto distribution (GPD)** as the threshold rises toward the right endpoint of the loss distribution. This follows from an important limit theorem in EVT. For details, the reader is referred to *McNeil, Frey, and Embrechts (2005)*. The cumulative distribution function of GPD is the following:

$$G_{\xi,\beta}(y) = \begin{bmatrix} 1 - (1 + xy/\beta)^{1/x}, & x \neq 0 \\ 1 - \exp(-y/\beta), & x = 0 \end{bmatrix}$$

Here $\xi$ is generally referred to as the shape parameter and $\beta$ as the scale parameter.

Though strictly speaking, the GPD is only the *limiting* distribution for excess losses over a high threshold, however, it serves as the natural model of the excess loss distribution even for finite thresholds. In other words, for a high enough threshold, the excess distribution can already be considered close enough to GPD, so that the latter can be used as a model for the excess distribution. Essentially, we assume that

$$F_u(y) = G_{\xi,\beta}(y)$$

for some $\xi$ and $\beta$.

Once a GPD is fitted to excess losses, it may be used among others to calculate high quantiles (Value at Risk) and conditional expectations for the original loss distribution. Specifically, the loss distribution function is modeled over the threshold $u$ as

$$F(x) = \left[1 - F(u)\right] \cdot G_{\xi,\beta}(x-u) + F(u)$$

with $F(u)$ typically estimated empirically. This represents a parametric model for the tail of the original loss distribution above the threshold.

# Application – modeling insurance claims

In the remainder of this chapter, we work through an example of using EVT in a real-life risk management application. We apply the preceding methodology to fire insurance claims, with the aims of fitting a distribution to the tails and providing quantile estimates and conditional expectations to characterize the probability and magnitude of large fire losses. We note that the exact same steps may be applied to credit losses or operational losses as well. For market risk management problems, where the underlying data is generally the return of a security, we would remove the gains from the data set and focus on the losses only; otherwise, the modeling steps are again identical.

Multiple packages are available in R for extreme value analysis. In this chapter we present the `evir` package in the following command. A good overview of the various R packages for EVT is provided in *Gilleland, Ribatet, and Stephenson (2013)*.

As done previously, we need to install and load the `evir` package before we use it:

```
> install.packages("evir")
> library(evir)
```

The data we use in this example consists of large industrial fire insurance claims from Denmark. The data set, covering the years from 1980 to 1990, contains all fire losses exceeding one million Danish krone. This is a popular data set often used in EVT for demonstration purposes. The data is available in the `evir` package; we can load it into our workspace using the following command:

```
> data(danish)
```

The resulting numeric vector contains 2,167 observations as well as the corresponding observation times. Type `help(danish)` for further details on the data set.

## Exploratory data analysis

To get some impression of the data, we calculate summary statistics and also plot the histogram of claims using the following commands:

```
> summary(danish)
   Min.  1st Qu.  Median   Mean  3rd Qu.   Max.
  1.000   1.321    1.778   3.385   2.967   263.300
> hist(danish, breaks = 200, xlim = c(0,20))
```

The following figure shows the histogram of Danish insurance claims.

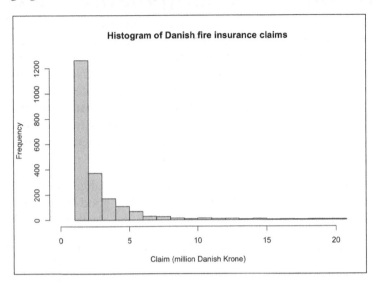

The distribution of claims is strongly skewed with a long-right tail, suggesting that small fire losses occur quite frequently; however, very large losses may occur occasionally as well (the largest claim in the data set is 263 million krone). These large claims are not even visible on the following histogram as we have truncated the plot at 20 million krone. As shown by the calculation in the following command lines, less than 2% of the losses are above this threshold, yet these represent 22% of the total loss amount:

```
> sum(danish>20) / length(danish)
[1] 0.01661283
> sum(danish[danish>20]) / sum(danish)
[1] 0.2190771
```

It is the probability of such extremely large losses occurring (as well as their expected magnitude) that we are interested in, in this example. Estimating such probabilities using relative frequencies of large losses in the sample is unreliable due to the small number of such losses.

# Tail behavior of claims

A perhaps more useful visualization of the data can be obtained using a *logarithmic scale* for the *x* axis (or even both axes). We perform this by plotting the empirical **complementary cumulative distribution function** (**ccdf**, that is, the empirical probability of the claims exceeding any given threshold, sometimes also referred to as the *survival function*) using the `emplot` function of the `evir` package. The following first command creates the plot using logarithmic scales on the x axis only, whereas the second command results in a plot with logarithmic scales on both axes:

```
> emplot(danish)
```

```
> emplot(danish, alog = "xy")
```

The following figure shows the second plot:

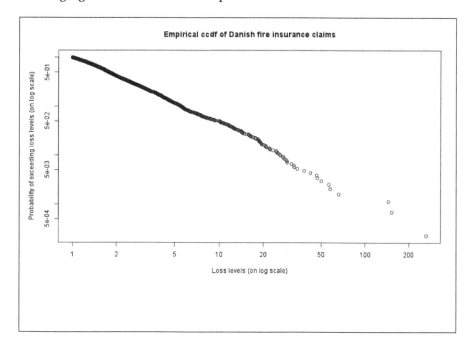

Interestingly, the empirical ccdf is nearly linear when plotted using logarithmic scales on both axes. This reveals the fat-tailed nature of the data and the possible Pareto-type distribution of the claims (also referred to as *power law*, as the ccdf can be written as a power of the thresholds).

Another useful tool to examine whether the data comes from a particular distribution is the **quantile-quantile plot (Q-Q plot)**. This plots quantiles of the data against quantiles of a hypothesized distribution. If the distribution assumption is correct, the resulting plot will be linear. Deviations from a linear plot reveal how the distribution of the data differs from the hypothesized distribution, for example, a concave plot indicates that the empirical distribution has a fatter tail.

Q-Q plots can be created using the `qplot` function of the `evir` package.

For loss data, the natural hypothesized distribution is the exponential distribution; consequently, the `qplot` function compares the data to the exponential distribution by default. The function, however, allows comparisons to be made to the more general GPD distribution by specifying its $\xi$ shape parameter via the argument `xi`. Additionally, the data can be right truncated at some value via the `trim` argument to avoid the largest observations distorting the plot. The following command creates a Q-Q plot of the Danish fire loss data against the exponential distribution, with the loss data truncated at 100:

```
> qplot(danish, trim = 100)
```

The resulting plot also confirms that the empirical distribution has a much fatter tail than the exponential distribution and so the latter is not a good model for the data.

# Determining the threshold

Now that we have established that the data is fat-tailed and follows a power law, we turn to fitting a GPD distribution to the threshold exceedances. However, before performing that, we need to determine an appropriate threshold. Though determining the threshold is at the discretion of the modeler, there exist useful tools that help to confirm that the convergence to GPD is already sufficient for a given threshold.

Perhaps the most useful tool for this is the **mean excess function**, defined as the average excess of the random variable $X$ over the threshold $u$, defined as a function of the threshold:

$$e(u) = E[X - u \mid X > u]$$

It can be easily shown that the mean excess function of the GPD is a linear function of the threshold $u$, with a coefficient proportional to the $\xi$ shape parameter of the distribution (accordingly, in general, a positive gradient of the mean excess function indicates fat tails, whereas a negative gradient indicates thin tails). Therefore, a reasonable way to determine the threshold is to find the value over which the sample mean excess function is approximately linear.

The meplot function of the evir package plots sample mean excesses over increasing thresholds. The omit argument allows you to specify the number of upper plotting points to be omitted from the plot (again, so that these points do not distort the plot).

```
> meplot(danish, omit = 4)
```

The following figure shows the resulting sample mean excess plot:

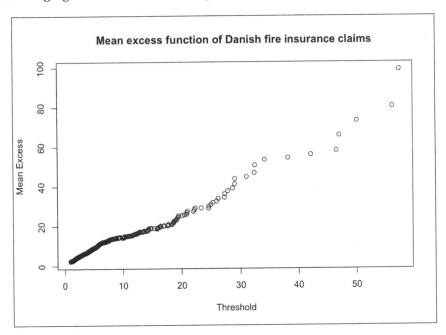

The resulting plot looks fairly linear across the whole spectrum of losses; consequently, it might even be possible to fit a single GPD distribution to the entire data set. However, we may observe a small kink just below 10, possibly indicating that smaller losses follow a somewhat different law. A fairly linear region can be observed between 10 and 20; above 20 the data becomes sparse. Therefore, a threshold of 10 can be considered a reasonable choice that is consistent with the sample mean excess function. This leaves us with 109 losses exceeding this threshold (5% of the original sample).

# Fitting a GPD distribution to the tails

Now we have everything ready to fit a GPD distribution to the tails of the fire loss data. We can perform the fitting using the gpd function, specifying the threshold determined in the preceding section, using the following command:

```
> gpdfit <- gpd(danish, threshold = 10)
```

The gpd function uses the **maximum likelihood (ML)** method by default to estimate the parameters of the GPD distribution. The function returns an object of the gpd class, containing the estimated parameters (together with their standard errors and covariances) as well as the data exceeding the specified threshold. The zero value of the converged member indicates convergence to the maximum in case ML estimation was used. The members par.ests and par.ses contain the estimated $\xi$ and $\beta$ parameters and their standard errors, respectively.

```
> gpdfit$converged
[1] 0
> gpdfit$par.ests
      xi      beta
0.4968062 6.9745523
> gpdfit$par.ses
      xi      beta
0.1362093 1.1131016
```

Our ML estimation thus resulted in the estimated parameters of $\xi = 0.50$ and $\beta = 6.97$, with standard errors of 0.14 and 1.11, respectively.

To verify our results, we may use the plot(gpdfit) command that provides a menu for plotting the empirical distribution of excesses and the tail of the original distribution (along with the fitted GPD), as well as a scatterplot and a Q-Q plot of the residuals from the fit. The following figure shows the excess distribution and fitted GPD distribution (plot 1 from the menu) — the GPD distribution clearly provides a very good fit to the data:

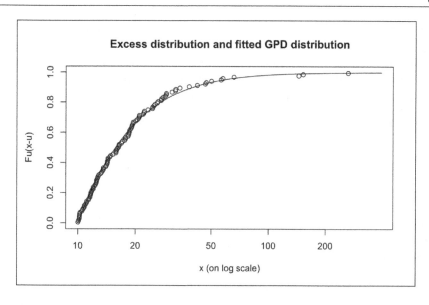

**Excess distribution and fitted GPD distribution**

x (on log scale)

# Quantile estimation using the fitted GPD model

Now that we have fitted a GPD model to the data, we can use it to estimate high quantiles or **Value at Risk (VaR)**. We can do this using the gpd.q function, which however needs a list object returned from plot.gpd or the tailplot function (which corresponds to selection 2 of the plot.gpd menu). We use the tailplot function to directly create a plot of the tail of the original Danish fire loss distribution. We then pass in the returned object to gpd.q, along with the pp argument specifying the quantile to be estimated.

```
> tp <- tailplot(gpdfit)
> gpd.q(tp, pp = 0.999, ci.p = 0.95)
 Lower CI  Estimate  Upper CI
 64.66184  94.28956 188.91752
```

The estimated 99.9% quantile is 94.29 million Danish krone. As there are only three observations exceeding this level, had we estimated this quantile from the empirical distribution, our estimate would have been quite prone to error. As a comparison, the standard empirically estimated quantile, obtained using the `quantile` function, results in an estimated 99.9% quantile of 144.66 million Danish krone:

```
> quantile(danish, probs = 0.999, type = 1)
   99.9%
144.6576
```

Essentially, the standard quantile estimation is driven by the single data point 144.6576 (corresponding to the third largest loss in the data set). EVT fills the data gap with a parametric form for the tail to provide a more reliable estimate. This is especially useful in operational risk applications where regulations require the calculation of a very high quantile (99.9%).

In addition to calculating the estimated quantile and its confidence intervals (whose probability is specified by the `ci.p` argument), the `gpd.q` function also adds an overlay to the tail distribution plot produced by `tailplot`, displaying the point estimate for the quantile (vertical dashed line), and the profile likelihood curve of the estimator (dashed curve). The boundaries of the confidence interval for the estimation are given by the intersections of the dashed curve and the horizontal dashed line, as shown in the following figure:

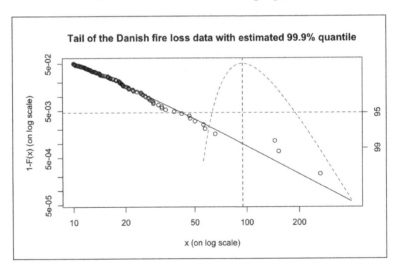

# Calculation of expected loss using the fitted GPD model

The fitted GPD model might also be used to estimate the expected size of insurance loss, given that a certain level of loss is exceeded. Alternatively, we may want to estimate the expected loss given that a particular quantile of the loss (for example, the 99% quantile) is exceeded. In risk management, the latter measure is called **Expected Shortfall (ES)**. The following commands calculate the 99% Expected Shortfall using the `gpd.sfall` function:

```
> tp <- tailplot(gpdfit)
> gpd.q(tp, pp = 0.99)
Lower CI Estimate Upper CI
23.36194 27.28488 33.16277
> gpd.sfall(tp, 0.99)
 Lower CI  Estimate  Upper CI
 41.21246  58.21091 154.88988
```

The estimated 99% quantile is 27.28 million Danish krone and the estimated 99% Expected Shortfall is 58.21 million Danish krone. In other words, assuming that the 99% quantile level of 27.28 million is exceeded, the expected loss is 58.21 million. The following graph shows the estimate of 99% Expected Shortfall for Danish fire loss data.

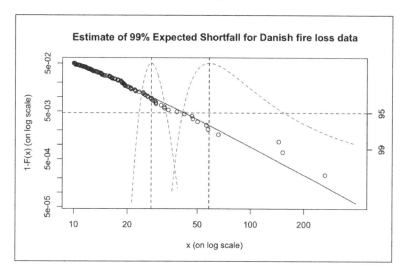

The resulting graph displays both the 99% quantile or VaR (first vertical dashed line and corresponding profile likelihood curve) and the 99% Expected Shortfall (second vertical dashed line and corresponding profile likelihood curve).

# Summary

In this chapter, we presented a case study of how Extreme Value Theory methods can be used in R in a real-life risk management application. After briefly covering the theory of threshold exceedance models in EVT, we worked through a detailed example of fitting a model to the tails of the distribution of fire insurance claims. We used the fitted model to calculate high quantiles (Value at Risk) and conditional expectations (Expected Shortfall) for the fire losses. The presented methods are readily extendable to market, credit, or operational risk losses as well.

# 9
# Financial Networks

We have seen in the previous chapter how extreme events coming from asymmetric and fat-tailed distributions can be modeled and how the risk associated with extreme events can be measured and managed.

In some cases we have access to financial data that enables us to construct complex networks. In financial networks, it is quite usual that the distribution of some attributes (degree, quantity, and so on) is highly asymmetric and fat-tailed too.

By nature, available financial networks are usually not complete; they do not contain either all possible players, or all possible connections, or all relevant attributes. But even in their limited state, they constitute an extremely rich and informative data set which can help us to get insight into the detailed microstructure of the market under investigation.

This chapter gives an overview of how financial networks can be represented, simulated, visualized, and analyzed in R. We will focus on two important practical problems:

- How topology changes of the network can be detected
- How systemically important players can be identified with the help of centrality measures

# Representation, simulation, and visualization of financial networks

Networks can be represented by a list of pairs, by an adjacency matrix, or by graphs. Graphs consist of vertices and edges (nodes). In R, vertices are numbered and may have several attributes. Between two vertices there can exist an edge (directed or undirected, weighted or non-weighted), and the edge may have other attributes as well. In most financial networks, vertices stand for market players, while edges describe different sorts of financial linkages between them.

Using the built-in R tools and some function from the `igraph` package, it is easy to create/simulate artificial networks. The following table (Table 1) summarizes some important network types and their basic properties:

| Network | Clustering | Average path length | Degree distribution |
| --- | --- | --- | --- |
| **Regular** (for example, ring, full) | High | High | Equal or fixed in-out degrees in each node |
| **Pure random** (for example, Erdős-Rényi) | Low | Low | Exponential, Gaussian |
| **Scale free** | Variable | Variable | Power law/fat-tail |
| **Small world** (for example, Barabási, Watz-Strogatz) | High | Low | Power law/fat-tail |

Table 1: Properties of networks

The source of this table is *Markose at al. 2009*.

The most important network properties are the following:

- Density measures the extent of links between nodes relative to all possible links in a complete graph.
- Clustering (called transitivity in R) measures how interconnected each agent's neighbors are and is considered to be the hallmark of social networks. The clustering coefficient for the entire network is the average of all coefficients for its nodes.
- Path length is the distance between two agents and is given by the number of edges that separate them; the average of the shortest paths characterizes the whole network. The longest shortest path in the network is called diameter.
- Degree is the number of connections the node has to other nodes. Degree distribution is the probability distribution of these degrees over the whole network.

*Non-random regular networks* are highly ordered where each node connects to all of its nearest neighbors. A full graph can be generated with the `igraph` package's `graph.full`, and partial networks can be generated with a similar function resulting in tree, lattices, ring, and so on.

In contrast to regular networks, in a *pure random Erdős-Rényi network*, linkages are generated by choosing two nodes uniformly at random. As we are dealing with random numbers here, it is worth setting a custom seed and the state of the random number generator, so that it would return the same random number in all R sessions.

```
> set.seed(7)
```

When simulating an Erdős-Rényi graph, we have to set at least two parameters in advance: the number of the nodes (for example, 100) and the probability for drawing an edge between two arbitrary vertices (for example, 0.1):

```
> e <- erdos.renyi.game(100, 0.1)
> plot(e)
```

The following figure depicts a pure random network (Erdős-Rényi):

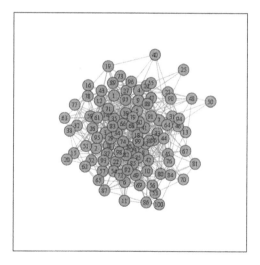

We can also calculate the main characteristics of the preceding network, which are density, clustering (transitivity), and average path length, from Table 1:

```
> graph.density(e)
[1] 0.05434343
> transitivity(e)
[1] 0.05522828
> average.path.length(e)
[1] 2.923636
```

Graph density and transitivity are around 0.1, the initially-set edge probability and the difference is only due to the noise inherent in the small sample.

In a *scale-free network*, degree distribution follows a power law; therefore vertices differ enormously in terms of their degree. *Small-world networks* constitute a special subset of scale-free networks where vertices tend to form cliques, resulting in the overabundance of weakly-linked dense hubs. Not surprisingly, clustering coefficient is remarkably high and average path is short in small-world networks. Preferential attachment and fitness have been proposed as mechanisms to explain power law degree distributions and clustering; see *Barabási-Albert (1999)* and *Bianconi-Barabási (2001)*. Social/financial networks are often modeled as small world. There are several ways of creating small world networks in R, for example, `watts.strogatz.game` or `barabasi.game`. Let us use the first one here:

```
> set.seed(592)
> w <- watts.strogatz.game(1, 100, 5, 0.05)
> plot(w)
```

The following figure depicts a random scale-free network (Watts-Strogatz):

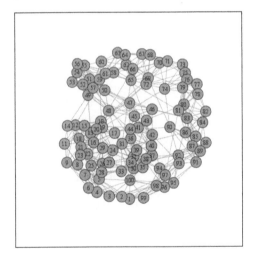

Let us compare our Watts-Strogatz small-world network to the previous pure random Erdős-Rényi graph in terms of the main network measures:

```
> graph.density(w)
[1] 0.1010101            # approximately the same
> transitivity(w)
[1] 0.4626506            # much higher
> average.path.length(w)
[1] 2.625455             # longer
```

In the preceding R chunk, we have stored the result of the Watts-Strogatz game in a variable called b that we plotted afterwards. Extracting the list of edges can be done easily with the `get.edgelist` function that would return a matrix of two columns. Here we show only the first five rows of the returned list:

```
> we <- get.edgelist(w) > head(we, 5)
      [,1] [,2]
[1,]    1    2
[2,]    2   77
[3,]    3    4
[4,]    4    5
[5,]    5    6
```

Other network manipulations are also possible in R. For example, we may wish to see the adjacency matrix of the graph with the help of the `get.adjacency` function. Or, it can be useful to randomize our network by permuting vertex IDs, which can be done with `permute.vertices`. It can happen that we need to merge several vertices into one along with some vertex attributes by using `contract.vertices`. We can also create the `union` and `intersection` of several networks with some internal R functions named accordingly.

# Analysis of networks' structure and detection of topology changes

Now, let us suppose we have access to a real-world database of an interbank market (randomized data for illustrative purpose), where banks lend to each other and lending banks report on their positions at the end of each day in the period of 2007-2010. The database consists of 50 banks and the maturity of the loans is one day. In order to manipulate the real-world networks in R, it is advisable to convert our data into a CSV file and save it into our working directory. The following table (Table 2) shows the top lines of our CSV file:

| Bank | Partner | Amount | Interest | Year | Month | Day |
|------|---------|--------|----------|------|-------|-----|
| 1 | 21 | 5 | 7,9 | 2007 | 1 | 3 |
| 1 | 42 | 3 | 7,9 | 2007 | 1 | 3 |
| 10 | 11 | 0,35 | 7,8 | 2007 | 1 | 3 |
| 18 | 24 | 2 | 8 | 2007 | 1 | 3 |
| 2 | 11 | 1,3 | 7,8 | 2007 | 1 | 3 |
| 21 | 11 | 0,8 | 7,8 | 2007 | 1 | 3 |
| 21 | 2 | 5 | 7,75 | 2007 | 1 | 3 |
| 3 | 24 | 4 | 7,95 | 2007 | 1 | 3 |

Table 2: Database of an interbank market

Source: The authors

Each row contains a transaction: the reporting bank (the lender), its partner bank (the borrower), the loan amount, the interest rate, and the date of the transaction. We can read these details in our data from the CSV file:

```
> data <- read.csv2('networktable.csv')
```

Now we have a table of seven columns and 21,314 rows:

```
> str(data)
'data.frame':   21314 obs. of  7 variables:
 $ Bank    : int  1 1 10 18 2 21 21 3 3 30 ...
 $ Partner : int  21 42 11 24 11 11 2 24 42 12 ...
 $ Amount  : num  5 3 0.35 2 1.3 0.8 5 4 1.8 2 ...
 $ Interest: num  7.9 7.9 7.8 8 7.8 7.8 7.75 7.95 7.9 7.9 ...
 $ Year    : int  2007 2007 2007 2007 2007 2007 2007 2007 2007 ...
 $ Month   : int  1 1 1 1 1 1 1 1 1 1 ...
 $ Day     : int  3 3 3 3 3 3 3 3 3 3 ...
```

The size of the balance sheet of each bank is also available and is stored in a separate CSV file. The first column of the CSV file is assumed to contain symbolic vertex names, other columns will be added as additional vertex attributes.

```
> size <- read.csv2('vertices.csv')
```

We can create graph objects using our data frames in the following way:

```
> bignetwork <- graph.data.frame(data, vertices = size)
```

This function creates an `igraph` object. The data frames must contain the edge list in the first two columns. Additional columns are considered as edge attributes.

In the second step we can ask for the network's basic properties.

```
> is.connected(bignetwork)
[1] TRUE
```

The network is fully connected, meaning that during 2007-2010 all the banks traded with all the other banks at least once. We can check whether the network has multiple edges:

```
> table(is.multiple(bignetwork))
FALSE   TRUE
 1049 20265
```

R found many edges that are multiple, meaning that banks traded several times with the same partners. Let us also check whether the network has loops, that is, transactions where the reporting bank and the partner bank was the same:

```
> str(is.loop(bignetwork))
logi [1:21314] FALSE FALSE FALSE FALSE FALSE FALSE ...
```

Here we get a list of all the edges. It seems that there are some loops which must be data errors. If we wish to leave out all the loops and summarize the multiple edges, we can do it in one step by simplifying the network:

```
> snetwork <- simplify(bignetwork, edge.attr.comb = "sum")
```

Having our graph simplified, we can plot it with relatively small arrows not to overcrowd the resulting figure:

```
> plot(snetwork, edge.arrow.size = 0.4)
```

The following figure depicts our real-world network:

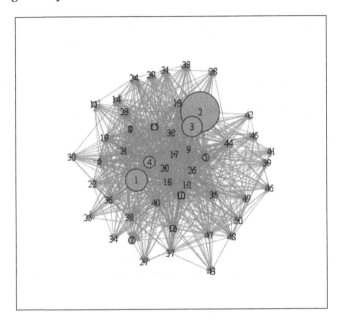

In the third step, we can apply complex analytical tools built in R to explore the inner structure of the network.

Communities (densely connected subgraphs) can be detected, for example, by the `walktrap.community` function, which finds densely connected subgraphs. The idea is that short random walks tend to stay in the same community.

Modularity is the share of the edges belonging to the given groups minus the expected share, if edges were distributed at purely random. Modularity ranges between [−1/2,1). If it is positive, it is the sign of clustering.

```
> communities
Number of communities (best split): 2
Modularity (best split): 0.02499471
Membership vector:
 1  2  3  4  5  6  7  8  9 10 11 12 13 14 15 16 17 18 19 20 21 22 23
 1  1  1  1  1  1  1  1  1  1  1  1  1  1  1  1  1  1  1  1  1  1  1
24 25 26 27 28 29 30 31 32 33 34 35 36 37 38 39 40 41 42 43 44 45 46
 1  1  1  1  1  1  1  1  1  1  1  1  1  1  1  1  1  2  1  2  1  2  2
47 48 49 50
 2  2  2  2
```

Besides the properties presented in Table 1 (density, transitivity, average path, and degree distribution), many other R functions can also be applied to characterize our network, for example, `graph.coreness`, `girth`, `cliques.number`, `reciprocity`, and so on. Further details can be found in the official igraph manual available at:

```
http://igraph.sourceforge.net/doc/html/
```

The market structures evolve in time. They show high stability in peacetime, meaning that regardless of numerous alterations, their fundamental topology remains the same, for example, see *Lublóy (2006)*. But fundamental changes may occur in times of crisis: markets dry out and refill, the number and the market share of active players change dramatically, and the role of the players may also change (for example, lenders become borrowers and vice versa), see for example, *Soramäki et al. (2006)* and *Bech-Atalay (2008)*.

The default Lehman Brothers was announced on September 15, 2008 which had a deep impact on financial markets all around the world. Hence, it seems reasonable to compare network topologies before and after this event. In order to detect the fundamental changes in the topology, let us first create a series of monthly aggregated networks, then calculate network measures for each month and plot them as time series.

To match only a part of the data, the `subset` function can be useful. For example, to filter September of 2008 one may run:

```
> monthlynetwork <- subset(data, (Year == 2008) & (Month == 9))
```

In the next few examples we will iteratively subset a month of the original dataset and will also apply some functions on the subsets. This can be done with a basic loop, with different `apply` functions (especially `ddply` from the `plyr` package), or by aggregating the dataset by given dimensions. We start from aggregate measures and gradually zoom into details. Hence, let us see first, how aggregate quantity (sum of amounts in a month) changed over time:

```
> mAmount <- with(data,
+    aggregate(Amount, by = list(Month = Month, Year = Year),
+    FUN = sum))
```

Here we have computed the sum of Amount in each Year and Month inside of data with the help of the `aggregate` command. Let us also `plot` the results as a monthly time series, using the following command:

```
> plot(ts(mAmount$x, start = c(2007, 1), frequency = 12),
+    ylab = 'Amount')
```

The following figure depicts the evolution of the monthly amount over time:

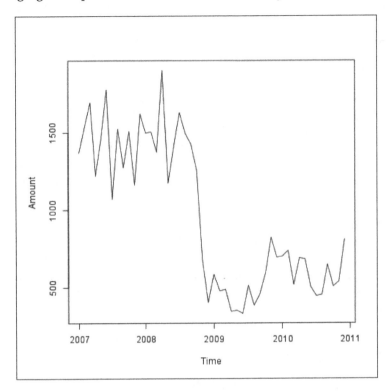

On the above figure we can observe an important structural change just after the Lehman-fall. If we have a closer look at the network, it turns out that the inner structure of the network has also dramatically changed after the burst of the crisis. In order to demonstrate these changes, we can calculate and plot network measures month to month as time series. We calculate the case of graph density with a nested loop, computing the values for each month.

```
> ds <- sapply(2007:2010, function(year) {
+     sapply(1:12, function(month) {
+         mdata <- subset(data, (Year == year) & (Month == month))
+         graph.density(graph.data.frame(mdata))
+     })
+})
> plot(ts(as.vector(ds), start = c(2007, 1), frequency=12))
> abline(v = 2008 + 259/366, col = 'red')
```

The following figure depicts the evolution of graph density over time:

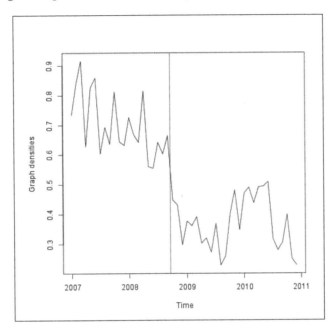

We can see that after the Lehman-fall network density suddenly dropped, reflecting that transactions concentrated on fewer banks, most of the other network measures showed significant structural changes as well.

# Contribution to systemic risk – identification of SIFIs

A complex system is not simply the sum of its elements. It is possible that all entities are safe in themselves, but the system as a whole is still vulnerable. Systemic risk is the risk of the entire system collapsing due to one or several shocks. If we wish to identify the **systemically important financial institutions (SIFIs)** as it was proposed by BCBS (2011), we have to consider five factors contributing to systemic risk: size, interconnectedness, lack of substitutes, cross-jurisdictional activity, and complexity of the activities. When measuring interconnectedness, we can rely on network data and can apply several methods, for example, centrality measures, stress test, and core-periphery models.

Now, we illustrate the first method based on an index of some centrality measures, as described in *Komárková et al.(2012)* and *von Peter (2007)*. Banks with the highest index-value can be considered as the most central ones, thus with the most SIFIs. Simpler centrality measures are based on fairly narrow information set containing only connections and directions, while edge weights and other attributes are completely set aside. For example, simpler centrality measures are as follows:

- **Degree (in/out/all)**: It shows the total number of incoming, outcoming, and all transactions where the bank was involved in.

- **Betweenness (directed/undirected)**: It shows the frequency with which a bank lies on the shortest path. When determining the shortest path, the network can be treated as directed or undirected. In the first case the shortest path is longer, therefore frequency is higher.

- **Closeness (in/out/all)**: It is the average of the reciprocal of the length of all shortest paths to other banks. This measure helps to identify banks with the broadest reach to other banks, including the smallest ones.

- **Eigenvector (in/out/all)**: It is the measure of how well a given bank is connected to other well-connected banks.

Let us take the period of 2007 to 2010 as a whole and concentrate on all the connections in a directed graph using the following command:

```
> g <- graph.data.frame(data)
```

We calculate the four preceding centrality measures and aggregate them into an index.

```
> degree <- degree(g, normalized = TRUE)
> between <- betweenness(g, normalized = TRUE)
> closeness <- closeness(g, normalized = TRUE)
> eigenv <- evcent(g, directed = TRUE)$vector
```

When computing the index, we have to normalize the difference of the centrality measure of a given bank to the mean of the centrality measure over the whole population. For this end, we can construct a function if we do not want to use the built-in `scale` with various options:

```
> norm <- function(x) x / mean(x)
```

If centrality measures are equally weighted, we will use the following formula:

```
> index <- (norm(degree) + norm(between) +
+  norm(closeness) + norm(eigenv)) / 4
> index
          1          8         15          2         18          3
0.91643667 0.49431153 1.06216769 1.35739158 4.56473014 1.44833480
         26         32         35         36         37          4
1.36048296 0.73206790 1.13569863 0.40296085 0.54702230 3.94819802
```

Now, we plot the distribution of the index and select the banks with the highest index value, as shown in the following figure, generated using the following command:

```
> hist(index)
```

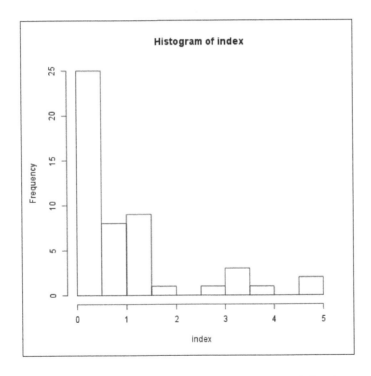

Once we have the index distribution, we have to decide which banks we consider important (for example, banks with index value higher than 2.5: 18, 12, 20, 17, 9, and 10). Of course, the index could be completed with other centrality measures, that is, more advanced ones relying on broader information set; see for example, intermediacy in *von Peter (2007)*.

# Summary

In this chapter, we focused on financial networks and used the `igraph` package of R, which provided effective tools for network simulation, manipulation, visualization, and analysis. We learned how to read in network data and how to explore the network's basic properties. We discovered that our illustrative market data exhibited significant structural changes due to the crisis. In the final part we showed a simple method of finding systematically important players within the network.

# References

## Time series analysis

- G. E. P. Box and G. M. Jenkins (1976), *Time Series Analysis: Forecasting and Control*. Holden-Day, San Francisco.

- R. F. Engle (1982), *Autoregressive Conditional Heteroscedasticity with Estimates of the Variance of U.K. Inflation*, Econometrica 50, 987-1007.

- C. W. J. Granger (1981), *Some Properties of Time Series Data and Their Use in Econometric Model Specification*, Journal of Econometrics 16, 121-130.

- R. F. Engle and C. W. J. Granger (1987), *Co-Integration and Error Correction: Representation, Estimation, and Testing*, Econometrica 55, No. 2, 251-276.

- R. F. Engle and B. S. Yoo (1987), *Forecasting and Testing in Co-Integrated Systems*, Journal of Econometrics 35, 143-159.

## Portfolio optimization

- P. Carl and B.G. Peterson (2013), *PerformanceAnalytics: Econometric Tools for Performance and Risk Analysis*. Available at http://cran.r-project.org/package=PerformanceAnalytics.

- R. McTaggart and G. Daróczi (2013), *Quandl: Quandl Data Connection*. Available at http://cran.r-project.org/package=Quandl.

- R. C. Merton (1993), *On the Microeconomic Theory of Investment under Uncertainty*, Handbook of Mathematical Economics, in: K. J. Arrow and M.D. Intriligator (ed.), Handbook of Mathematical Economics, edition 4, volume 2, chapter 13, 601-669, Elsevier.

- J.A. Ryan (2013), *quantmod: Quantitative Financial Modelling Framework*. Available at http://cran.r-project.org/package=quantmod.

- A. Trapletti and K. Hornik (2013), tseries: *Time Series Analysis and Computational Finance*. Available at `http://cran.r-project.org/package=tseries`.

- W. F. Sharpe (1964), *Capital Asset Prices: A Theory of Market Equilibrium under Conditions Of Risk, Journal of Finance, American Finance Association 19, No. 3, 425-442, 09.*

- D. Wuertz and M. Hanf (2010), *Portfolio Optimization with R/Rmetrics (Rmetrics Association & Finance Online)* Available at `www.rmetrics.org`.

- D. Wuertz and Y. Chalabi (2013), timeSeries: *Rmetrics - Financial Time Series Objects.* Available at `http://cran.r-project.org/package=timeSeries`.

# Asset pricing

- Z. Bodie, A. Kane, and A. Marcus (2004), *Investments, Edition 6, McGraw-Hill Irwin.*

- J. H. Cochrane (2005), *Asset pricing, Princeton University Press, New Jersey.*

- J. Lintner (1965), *Security Prices, Risk, and Maximal Gains from Diversification, Journal of Finance 20, No. 4, 587-615.*

- J. Lintner (1965), *The Valuation of Risk Assets and the Selection of Risky Investments in Stock Portfolios and Capital Budget, Review of Economics and Statistics 47, No. 1, 13-37.*

- P. Medvegyev and J. Száz (2010), *A meglepetések jellege a pénzügyi piacokon. Bankárképző, Budapest.*

- M. Miller and M. Scholes (1972), *Rates of Return in Relation to Risk: A Re-examination of Some Recent Findings, in: Studies in the Theory of Capital Markets, New York, Praeger, 47-78.*

- S. A. Ross (1976), *Return, Risk and Arbitrage, in: Risk and Return in Finance, Cambridge, Mass, Ballinger.*

- W. F. Sharpe (1964), *Capital Asset Prices: A Theory of Market Equilibrium Under Conditions of Risk, Journal of Finance 19, No. 3, 425-442.*

- P. Wilmott (2007), *Paul Wilmott Introduces Quantitative Finance, Edition 2, John Wiley & Sons Ltd, West Sussex.*

# Fixed income securities

- J. C. Hull (2012), *Options, Futures, and Other Derivatives, 8th edition, Prentice Hall.*

- Z. Bodie, A. Kane, and A. J. Marcus (2008), *Investments, 8th edition, McGraw-Hill.*

- *K. G. Nyborg (1996), The Use and Pricing of Convertible Bonds, Applied Mathematical Finance 3, No. 3, 167-190.*

- *M. J. Brennan and E. S. Schwartz (1980), Analyzing Convertible Bonds, Journal of Financial and Quantitative Analysis 15, 907-929. DOI: 10.2307/2330567.*

# Estimating the term structure of interest rates

- *J. H. McCulloch (1971), Measuring the Term Structure of Interest Rates, The Journal of Business 44, 19-31.*

- *J. H. McCulloch (1975), The Tax-Adjusted Yield Curve, The Journal of Finance 30, 811-830.*

- *R. Ferstl and J. Hayden (2010), Zero-Coupon Yield Curve Estimation with the Package termstrc, Journal of Statistical Software 36, No. 1, 1-34.*

# Derivatives Pricing

- *F. Black* and *M. Scholes (1973), The Pricing of Options and Corporate Liabilities, The Journal of Political Economy 81, No. 3, 637-654.*

- *J. Cox, S. Ross,* and *M. Rubinstein (1979), Option Pricing: A Simplified Approach, Journal of Financial Economics 7, No. 3, 229-263.*

- *D. Wuertz* and many others *(2012), fOptions: Basics of Option Valuation, R package version 2160.82.* Available at `http://CRAN.R-project.org/package=fOptions`.

- *R. C. Merton (1973), Theory of Rational Option Pricing, The Bell Journal of Economics and Management Science 4, No. 1, 141-183.*

- *R. Rebonato (1999), Volatility and Correlation, John Wiley, Chichester.*

- *S. Subramanian (2013), GUIDE: GUI for DErivatives in R, R package version 0.99.5.* Available at `http://CRAN.R-project.org/package=GUIDE`.

- *J. Hull (2011), Options, Futures, and Other Derivatives, Prentice Hall, 8th edition.*

# Credit risk management

- *F. Black* and *J. Cox (1976), Valuing Corporate Securities: Some Effects of Bond Indenture Provisions, Journal of Finance 31, 351-367.*

- *D. Wuertz* and many others *(2012), fOptions: Basics of Option Valuation, R package version 2160.82.* Available at `http://CRAN.R-project.org/package=fOptions`.

- K. Giesecke (2004), *Credit Risk Modeling and Valuation: An Introduction.* Available at SSRN: `http://ssrn.com/abstract=479323` or `http://dx.doi.org/10.2139/ssrn.479323`.

- I. Kojadinovic and J. Yan (2010), *Modeling Multivariate Distributions with Continuous Margins Using the copula R Package, Journal of Statistical Software 34, No. 9, 1-20.* Available at `http://www.jstatsoft.org/v34/i09`.

- J. Yan (2007), *Enjoy the Joy of Copulas: With a Package Copula, Journal of Statistical Software 21, No. 4, 1-21.* Available at `http://www.jstatsoft.org/v21/i04`.

- R. Merton (1974), *On the Pricing of Corporate Debt: The Risk Structure of Interest Rates, Journal of Finance. 29, 449-470.*

- D. Sharma (2011), *Innovation in Corporate Credit Scoring: Z-Score Optimization.* Available at SSRN: `http://ssrn.com/abstract=1963493` or `http://dx.doi.org/10.2139/ssrn.1963493`.

- S. M. Iacus (2009), *sde: Simulation and Inference for Stochastic Differential Equations, R package version 2.0.10.* Available at `http://CRAN.R-project.org/package=sde`.

- A. Wittmann (2007), *CreditMetrics: Functions for calculating the CreditMetrics risk model, R package version 0.0-2.*

- X. Robin, N. Turck, A. Hainard, N. Tiberti, F. Lisacek, J. C. Sanchez, and M. Müller (2011), *pROC: an open-source package for R and S+ to analyze and compare ROC curves, BMC Bioinformatics 12, 77.*

# Extreme value theory

- E. Gilleland, M. Ribatet, and A. G. Stephenson (2013), *A Software Review for Extreme Value Analysis, Extremes 16, 103-119.*

- A.J. McNeil, R. Frey, and P. Embrechts (2005), *Quantitative Risk Management, Princeton University Press, Princeton.*

# Financial networks

- A. L. Barabási and R. Albert (1999), *Emergence of scaling in random networks, Science 286, 509-512.*

- BCBS (2011), *Global Systemically Important Banks: Assessment Methodology and the Additional Loss Absorbency Requirement, Committee on Banking Supervision.* Available at `http://www.bis.org/publ/bcbs201.pdf`.

- M. L. Bech and E. Atalay (2008), *The topology of the federal funds market, Federal*

Reserve Bank of New York, Staff Reports, 354.

- *G. Bianconi* and *A. L. Barabási (2001), Competition and multiscaling in evolving networks, Europhysics Letters.54, 436.*

- *G. Csardi* and *T. Nepusz (2006), The igraph software package for complex network research, InterJournal, Complex Systems 1695.* Available at `http://igraph.sf.net`.

- *Z. Komárková, V. Hausenblas,* and *J. Frait (2012), How to Identify Systematically Important Financial Institutions, Report of the Central Bank of the Czech Republic, 100-111.*

- *Á. Lublóy (2006), Topology of the Hungarian large-value transfer system, MNB Occasional Papers, 57.*

- *S. Markose, S. Giansante, M. Gatkowski (2010),* and *A. R. Shaghaghi, Too-Interconnected-To-Fail: Financial Contagion and Systemic Risk in Network Model of CDS and Other Credit Enhancement Obligations of U.S. Banks, COMISEF Working Paper Series, WPS-033-21-04-2010.* Available at `http://comisef.eu/files/wps033.pdf` (downloaded on June 01, 2013).

- *K. Soramäki, M. L. Bech, J. Arnold, R. J. Glass,* and *W.E Beyeler (2006), The topology of interbank payment flows, Federal Reserve Bank of New York, Staff Reports, 243.*

- *G. von Peter (2007), International Banking Centers: a Network Perspective, BIS Quarterly Review.*

# Index

quantile estimation, fitted GPD model
used 121, 122
tail behavior claims 117, 118
threshold, determining 118, 119
**intensity models 106, 107**
**interest rates**
term structure, estimating 73, 74
**IT variable 33**

# L

**Lagrange Multiplier (LM) 20**
**Lagrange theorem 30, 31**
**lambda parameter 107**
**linear regression**
Beta estimation, using from 50-53
term structure, estimating by 75, 76
**linear time series**
forecasting 10
modeling 10
**loss given default (lgd) 111**

# M

**market portfolio.** *See* **tangency portfolio**
**market risk**
measuring, of fixed income security 64
**Market Risk Premium (MRP) 50**
**maximum likelihood (ML) 120**
**mean excess function 118**
**Mean-Variance model 29, 30**
**meplot function 119**
**migration matrices 111**
**min function 55**
**model**
diagnostic checking 12, 13
estimation 11, 12
forecasting 14
identification 11, 12
**model testing**
data collection 54-56
explanatory power, testing of individual
variance 59-61
SCL, modeling 57-59
**mod_static variable 18**

# N

**network structure**
analyzing 130-135
**net worth immunization 69**
**noise**
in covariance matrix 41

# O

**omit argument 119**
**Ordinary Least Squared (OLS) 50**

# P

**PerformanceAnalytics**
URL 139
**plot command 112**
**plot(gpdfit) command 120**
**Portfolio Frontier 36**
**Portfolio Optimization**
references 139, 140
with R/Rmetrics, URL 140
**prepro_bond function 78**
**priceyield function 66**

# Q

**qplot function 118**
**Quandl**
URL 32, 139
**Quandl function 33**
**quantile estimation**
fitted GPD model, using 121, 122
**quantile function 122**
**quantmod**
URL 139

# R

**R**
credit scoring 112
implementing in 65-68
**real data**
working with 32-39
**receiver operating characteristic (ROC) 100**

## Instant Oracle BPM for Financial Services How-to

ISBN: 978-1-78217-014-3        Paperback: 62 pages

Discover how to lavarage BPM in the financial sector

1. Learn something new in an Instant! A short, fast, focused guide delivering immediate results

2. Simplifies complex business problems for financial services

3. Optimize, enhance, and modify your business processes

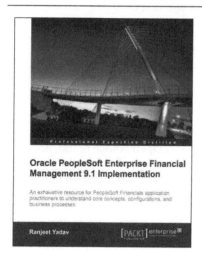

## Oracle PeopleSoft Enterprise Financial Management 9.1 Implementation

ISBN: 978-1-84968-146-9        Paperback: 412 pages

An exhaustive resource for PeopleSoft Financials application practitioners to understand core concepts, configurations, and business processes

1. A single concise book and eBook reference to guide you from PeopleSoft foundation concepts through to crucial configuration activities required for a successful implementation

2. Real-life implementation scenarios to demonstrate practical implementations of PeopleSoft features along with theoretical concepts

3. Expert tips for the reader based on wide implementation experience

Please check **www.PacktPub.com** for information on our titles

open source
community experience distilled

[PACKT]
PUBLISHING

## Haskell Financial Data Modeling and Predictive Analytics

ISBN: 978-1-78216-943-7  Paperback: 112 pages

Get an in-depth analysis of financial times series from the perspective of a functional programmer

1. Understand the foundations of financial stochastic processes

2. Build robust models quickly and efficiently

3. Tackle the complexity of parallel programming

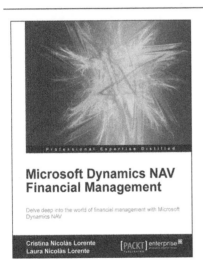

## Microsoft Dynamics NAV Financial Management

ISBN: 978-1-78217-162-1  Paperback: 134 pages

Delve deep into the world of financial management with Microsoft Dynamics NAV

1. Explore the features inside the sales and purchases areas as well as functionalities including payments, budgets, cash flow, fixed assets, and business intelligence

2. Discover how the different aspects of Dynamics NAV are related to financial management

3. Learn how to use reporting tools that will help you to make the right decisions at the right time

4. This book fully prepares you to successfully use Dynamics NAV as your key tool for financial management

Please check **www.PacktPub.com** for information on our titles

Lightning Source UK Ltd.
Milton Keynes UK
UKOW06f0147290714

235920UK00001B/34/P